TO:

FROM:

DATE:

BIBLE WISDOM FOR MEN

DEVOTIONS & PRAYERS

BARBOUR
PUBLISHING

Previously published as *Wise in the Word*.

ISBN 978-1-63609-175-4

Published by Barbour Publishing, Inc., 1810 Barbour Drive, Uhrichsville, Ohio 44683, www.barbourbooks.com

Our mission is to inspire the world with the life-changing message of the Bible.

ecpa Member of the Evangelical Christian Publishers Association

Printed in China.

BIBLE WISDOM FOR MEN:

DEVOTIONS & PRAYERS

This powerful devotional—written by and for men—will enhance your faith as you spend quiet time with key passages of scripture. One hundred Bible words or ideas—including *abundance*, *confidence*, *freedom*, *laughter*, *purpose*, *strength*, and *wonder*—form the basis of inspiring devotional readings. You'll be encouraged to think more deeply on the truth of God's unchanging Word—and the Lord's unending love for you.

HOPE

Be of good courage, and He shall strengthen your heart, all you who hope in the LORD.

PSALM 31:24 NKJV

In modern times, "hope" has been emasculated. We say things like "I hope the weather gets better," and we mean it would be nice if the sun came out soon. . .but we have no confidence that this will happen. We have turned hopes into wishes.

But when it comes to our experience with God, hope is much more than a wish. Biblical hope is simply waiting for God's promises to come to pass in His time. But, of course, waiting isn't easy.

David wrote Psalm 31 in the midst of great turmoil. He said, "I am forgotten like a dead man, out of mind; I am like a broken vessel. For I hear the slander of many; fear is on every side; while they take counsel together against me, they scheme to take away my life" (verses 12–13). And yet, as David faced this terror, he was confident that God wasn't going to abandon him.

It will take courage for us to have the kind of faith David did. This world will always try to turn believers away from God and His promises, so it requires an intentional effort to continue to believe. But when we do—when we have the "good courage" to "hope in the Lord"—God will strengthen our hearts and make our hopes secure.

Let this world have its wishes. We have confident hope in a loving God!

Lord, keep me from doubting Your promises. Make my hope in You as secure as David's, even when I am surrounded by the terrors of this world. Thank You for Your love and the strength that I can take from it.

TREASURE

"Lay up for yourselves treasures in heaven, where neither moth nor rust destroys and where thieves do not break in and steal."

MATTHEW 6:20 NKJV

What do you treasure? Maybe it's your car, your money, your house, or your fantasy football team. The reality is that you can't take any of those things with you when you die. And while you're alive, more often than not, they all just distract from the one thing that truly matters: your investment in the kingdom of God.

In Mark 10, Jesus met a young rich man who asked how to receive eternal life. Jesus told him to sell his possessions and give to the poor. The man walked away sad because he couldn't part with his treasure. But did Jesus' instruction end there?

After this interaction, Jesus told the disciples, "How hard it will be for those who have riches to enter the kingdom of God" (verse 23). He also said, "Many who are first will be last and the last first" (verse 31). Jesus' point was that God the Father doesn't take into account what you have accumulated on earth. He wants to see that you gave to the needy, fed the hungry, provided spiritual direction to the lost. That is your kingdom investment.

In Mark 10:29–30, Jesus promised, "There is no one who has left house or brothers or sisters or father or mother or wife or children or lands, for My sake and the gospel's, who shall not receive a hundredfold now in this time. . .and in the age to come, eternal life."

That's a treasure worth investing in!

Father, my possessions are worthless, but my investment in Your kingdom is priceless. Let my treasure be stored up in heaven not in the things of this world.

CHOICE

"You did not choose Me but I chose you, and appointed you that you would go and bear fruit, and that your fruit would remain, so that whatever you ask of the Father in My name He may give to you."

JOHN 15:16 NASB

It is 1954, just a couple of months before the U.S. Supreme Court's *Brown v. Board of Education* ruling outlaws segregation in public schools. In the Washington D.C. city basketball tournament for African-American schools, Armstrong Tech is facing Spingarn High, led by future NBA All-Star and Hall of Famer Elgin Baylor.

Baylor's team enters the game undefeated, but Armstrong Tech picks up the win, 50–47. Tech star Gary Mays holds Baylor to 18 points, less than half his seasonal average—and does so with *only one arm*. Mays, called "the One-Armed Bandit," had lost his left arm just below the shoulder in a childhood gun accident. But in spite of the disability, he grew up competing on the playgrounds of the national capital, where he had to prove he belonged.

"On the playgrounds, nobody would choose me until I beat them," Mays told a reporter for the sports website Deadspin. "So I had to beat them."

Isn't it good to know that we don't have to prove ourselves before Jesus will select us? He chooses and appoints whomever He pleases to go and bear spiritual fruit. If you've ever been rejected by other people, this is a humbling truth. It motivates us to live for Jesus, seeking opportunities to share the fruit of the Spirit with others who need an encounter with God.

Father, thank You for choosing me. Thank You for appointing me as Your representative to a world that often believes it must earn love and respect.

RIGHTEOUSNESS

For in the gospel the righteousness of God is revealed—a righteousness that is by faith from first to last, just as it is written: "The righteous will live by faith."

ROMANS 1:17 NIV

In modern parlance, a person who knows and acknowledges his own weakness and failure is said to have "self-awareness." A great biblical example of a self-aware man is the Old Testament prophet Isaiah.

God had specifically called Isaiah to speak to the wayward people of Judah. Yet when he came face-to-face with God, Isaiah could only cry out in woe, "I am ruined! For I am a man of unclean lips, and I live among a people of unclean lips, and my eyes have seen the King, the LORD Almighty" (Isaiah 6:5).

Isaiah understood something that each one of us must grasp: if we seek righteousness before a perfect God, we must first acknowledge our utter lack of it. As Isaiah wrote elsewhere, "All of us have become like one who is unclean, and all our righteous acts are like filthy rags" (Isaiah 64:6).

In the end, all of us must recognize that we have absolutely no ability to make ourselves "good enough" for God. We are only righteous before Him by placing our faith in the One He sent—Jesus, who lived on earth as a man and then died in our place. In His love, God made a way for us, a way we could never make for ourselves.

When we accept that by faith, God sees us as righteous.

Gracious, loving God, I know that in and of myself, I have no way to make myself righteous before You. Thank You, though, that You've made a way for me through Your Son, Jesus Christ.

CONFIDENCE

In the fear of the LORD *there is strong confidence.*
PROVERBS 14:26 NASB

The world considers the church to be a collection of weak-minded people who are foolish to fear the Lord. The unsaved don't believe in a personal God who loves His people. But you know better. You've experienced the refreshment of conversion. You've seen the Lord work mightily. You've read His Word and know it to be true. And as you've grown in your faith, the reality of today's verse has become more and more a part in your life.

That's probably what led Bible commentator Adam Clarke (1760–1832) to observe, "From genuine Christian experience, we find that the fear of God is highly consistent with the strongest confidence in his mercy and goodness."

In other words, fearing the Lord is a reverent love for what Christ has done for us on the cross, and as a result, the Christian finds strong confidence in such mercy and grace. Who else but God would go to such great lengths to express love for you? Hebrews 12:28–29 says it this way: "Since we receive a kingdom which cannot be shaken, let us show gratitude, by which we may offer to God an acceptable service with reverence and awe; for our God is a consuming fire."

If you had to give an honest assessment of your mindset in recent weeks, where would you say your confidence lies? Is it in your ability to secure wealth or maybe in your talents in general? Or is your confidence in your reverential awe of God?

Father, Proverbs 1:7 says, "The fear of the LORD is the beginning of knowledge." I also know it to be the source of my confidence. Grow my fear, Lord, that I may fully trust in You.

ABUNDANCE

Now to Him who is able to do far more abundantly beyond all that we ask or think, according to the power that works within us.

EPHESIANS 3:20 NASB

The website guinnessworldrecords.com tracks all kinds of records, including the largest collections belonging to single individuals. A man in the United Kingdom, for example, has a collection of 137 different traffic cones, representing over two-thirds of all known styles. A man in France owns the world's biggest private collection of jet fighters, with an amazing 110. In Northern California, someone claims to possess 500,000 unique pieces of *Star Wars* memorabilia, though "only" 93,260 have been audited and catalogued. We can certainly agree that these folks have an abundance of their favorite things.

When we hear the word *abundance*, our minds often think of wealth or possessions, and we're tempted to measure our own worth by material standards. But Christians possess so much more than "stuff."

The child of God enjoys grace, love, peace, and contentment, among a million other blessings. And these blessings are available in abundance. But how do we find them?

First, we need to recognize that physical things aren't the key to happiness. As Jesus once told a man who wanted his brother to divide an inheritance with him, "Beware, and be on your guard against every form of greed; for not even when one has an abundance does his life consist of his possessions" (Luke 12:15). Then align yourself with contented Christian people—the deep, peaceful, untroubled ones you see at church or Bible study—who enjoy the true spiritual abundance.

Let us strive for far more than just things.

Heavenly Father, help me to see my life through the abundance of gifts provided by the Holy Spirit.

MIRACLES

For no man can do these miracles that thou doest, except God be with him.
JOHN 3:2 KJV

Miracles come in all shapes and sizes. Desperately needed money might show up unexpectedly, or a life-saving organ arrives at the hospital just in the nick of time. Unfortunately, we often misplace the credit for these miracles. We chalk them up to luck or good fortune, or we say "karma" is paying us back. Luck, happily, has nothing to do with it. The author of miracles is God.

Perhaps the greatest miracle of all is spiritual rebirth through Jesus Christ. In Acts 10, we read of Cornelius, a Gentile soldier, and Peter, the well-known Jewish disciple of Jesus. One afternoon, God gave Cornelius a vision instructing him to send for the apostle. Peter also received a vision from God, instructing him never to call dirty anything God had cleaned.

When Peter arrived at Cornelius's place, he entered the house. That was a huge step for Peter, since Jews were prohibited from interacting with Gentiles. As Peter talked with Cornelius, the Holy Spirit fell upon all the Gentiles in the home. It was one of the greatest miracles ever recorded: Gentiles had been anointed, cleansed, and welcomed into the kingdom of God!

Not all miracles are this big or obvious. All miracles, though, are breathed out by God. No Magic 8 Ball can bring you your every desire. But God delivers what you need when you need it—even at times you may think it impossible.

Lord, I thank You for the many miracles You've done in my life. Many of them I may have not even noticed. But each and every one serves as a reminder that You are with me and care for me. Amen.

EXISTENCE

"For in him we live and move and exist. As some of your own poets have said, 'We are his offspring.'"

ACTS 17:28 NLT

Throughout human history, people have pondered their existence—why we're here and what that means. The seventeenth-century French mathematician and philosopher René Descartes gave voice to the certainty of our existence when he said, "I think, therefore I am."

The ability to think and reason—even to doubt—is certainly proof of one's own existence. But it doesn't answer the all-important questions of *how* and *why*. Those answers are found in the Word of God, which recounts the amazing story of creation in the first two chapters of Genesis. In that passage, we see God creating humans "in his image," meaning we are like Him in many important ways.

So that's the how. What about the why?

God, who is love (1 John 4:8), wanted to share that love with other beings. The apostle John marveled at the love God has for those He considers His "offspring." He wrote, "See what great love the Father has lavished on us, that we should be called children of God! And that is what we are!" (1 John 3:1 NIV).

God created people for much more than this life. He wanted us to live and move and exist in Him through His Son, Jesus Christ. That is the only existence worth having.

Are you one of His offspring?

God of love, I thank You for making me the way You did. Remind me often that my purpose in this life is to have fellowship with You—the way a child has fellowship with its loving father.

RECEIVE

The Lord *hath heard my supplication;*
the Lord *will receive my prayer.*
PSALM 6:9 KJV

In 1 Kings 18, we witness an epic standoff between God's prophet Elijah and the prophets of the false god Baal. Elijah challenges the 450 false prophets to call down fire from Baal to consume a sacrifice. When nothing occurs, Elijah askes God to do so—and He does.

Seeing this miracle, the people of Israel cry out, "The Lord, He is God!"

You might expect this to be a turning point in Israel's history, from unfaithfulness to obedience to the Lord. Unfortunately, just a few paragraphs later, we see Elijah himself, threatened by Queen Jezebel, fleeing for his life.

Elijah ran for an entire day, far into the desert. Once there, he prayed an honest prayer: "I have had enough, Lord," he said. "Take my life; I am no better than my ancestors" (1 Kings 19:4 NIV). Then he lay down under a tree and fell asleep.

Ever been here, where a sudden turn of events saps all your energy?

God "received" Elijah's prayer, answering by sending an angel. He touched the prophet's shoulder and said, "Get up and eat." There, in the middle of the desert, was some freshly baked bread and a jar of water. Elijah ate and drank and fell back asleep, and then the cycle repeated.

The Lord knew Elijah felt alone, frightened, and at the end of his strength. So in a stunning display of power and love, He let Elijah rest—then made him lunch and dinner!

Next time you reach the end of your earthly strength, cry out to God. He will hear and respond.

Lord, I thank You for receiving my prayers and answering in Your great power.

AUTHORITY

Every person is to be in subjection to the governing authorities. For there is no authority except from God, and those which exist are established by God.

ROMANS 13:1 NASB

Submission to governing authorities isn't difficult for believers—assuming that authority lines up with orthodox Christian views. But what happens when government leaders advocate positions that aren't biblical? What are Christians to do then?

The second portion of Romans 13:1 says all authority comes from and is established by God. . .even bad governments. Keep in mind that most of the rulers of the apostle Paul's day would have been far from Christian.

"The laws were made by pagans," said Bible commentator Albert Barnes, "and were adapted to the prevalence of paganism. Those kingdoms had been generally founded in conquest, and blood, and oppression. Many of the monarchs were blood-stained warriors; were unprincipled men; and were polluted in their private, and oppressive in their public, character."

Roman Christians, many of whom were converted Jews, had been under the heavy oppression of the empire for a long time. The notion of submitting to its authority would have been a tough pill to swallow, but Paul called for Christians to make submission their default setting.

There may be times when believers are called to stand against evil regimes in matters of life, conscience, and religious freedom. Since the first century, Christians have had to figure out when resistance is appropriate. Consider the apostles Peter and John telling the Jewish leadership, "We must obey God rather than men" (Acts 5:29).

But, generally speaking, submitting to governing authorities is the biblical rule. If you have questions, study this portion of scripture in depth and ask God for wisdom.

Father, may I view all governing authority as coming from You.

PERSEVERANCE

"You will be hated by everyone because of me, but the one who stands firm to the end will be saved."
MATTHEW 10:22 NIV

Paul Stutzman's excellent book *Biking Across America* could have been subtitled simply "Perseverance." It's the story of a middle-aged man who, after his wife's death from cancer, channeled his grief into a cross-country bicycle ride. While many have pedaled coast-to-coast in a group, with a support team, across the midsection of the United States, Stutzman rode entirely alone from the Pacific Northwest to Key West, Florida, a journey of nearly five thousand miles over sixty-nine days.

One particular slog highlights the perseverance required for the journey. After a hundred-mile ride through the hot Utah desert, Stutzman was disappointed to find no lodging at his intended stopping point. Impulsively, at 6 p.m., he set out for another town in hopes of finding a hot shower and comfortable bed. As things turned out, that was almost as far as he had already ridden! Stutzman pedaled 180 miles over twenty-five hours before he finally took his rest.

Few of us would attempt such an incredible physical journey, but know this: life will place similar demands on our emotional strength and stamina. Our jobs, marriages, children, temptations—even our decision to follow Jesus—will at times place an almost unbearable strain on our spirit. But Jesus' command (with a promise) is "persevere." Stand firm to the end and be saved.

If that seems easier said than done, remember that God simply wants your willingness—and He will provide the strength. To paraphrase the apostle Paul in Ephesians 3:16:

I pray that out of God's glorious riches He may strengthen me with power through His Spirit in my inner being, so that Christ may dwell in my heart through faith.

GRACE

For by grace are ye saved through faith.
EPHESIANS 2:8 KJV

People. . .enough said.

The American sage Mark Twain is often credited with the saying "The more I learn about people, the more I like my dog." If you've ever had a good dog, you know exactly what he was talking about. It's the same point that cartoonist Gary Larson illustrated in *The Far Side*: a dog chained to a docked Viking ship wags his tail eagerly as the crew returns from plundering. A dog doesn't care what kind of person you are—he just loves you. He shows you grace.

Pastors often describe this biblical concept as "unmerited favor"—goodness and blessing that we don't deserve. Not even a little bit.

Do you recall that Jesus spoke a lot about forgiveness? That's because He knew how much we'd need it. And He knew we'd need a way to give this grace to others. The Bible says Jesus was tempted in every way and yet did not sin (Hebrews 4:15). That temptation included the desire to pay others back for the wrong they'd done.

Did someone get on your last nerve again today? Is there someone who continually, maliciously, enjoys making your life miserable? When you're tempted to lash out, remember your dog. He knows exactly who you are, and he loves you anyway. He's actually *happy* to see you. That's just who he is. Why? Because grace is something you give.

When we're wronged in any way, Jesus only gives us one option: grace. "Father, forgive them; for they know not what they do" (Luke 23:34).

Jesus, today when I am offended, give me the grace to spread out my arms as You did, to forgive completely, and to allow You to make all things new.

HOME

"In My Father's house are many mansions; if it were not so, I would have told you. I go to prepare a place for you. And if I go and prepare a place for you, I will come again and receive you to Myself; that where I am, there you may be also."

JOHN 14:2–3 NKJV

Turn the clock back two thousand years and imagine that you are one of Jesus' disciples. You walk with Christ, see His miracles, hear His teaching. He talks about the kingdom of God, and you wait for Him to take His place as its rightful king. Then you hear Jesus say that He's leaving.

How would you feel? Abandoned?

Jesus' disciples did feel that way, which is why Jesus revealed His plan in John 14. He isn't leaving them without purpose. He's leaving to prepare a place for them. Jesus is going to get their home ready.

For Christians, home isn't the house we live in or the town where we grew up. Our home is with Christ.

That's why we long for things that this world simply can't provide. This world isn't our home.

When Christ ascended into heaven, He didn't leave us homeless here on earth. When we are saved by faith, Jesus doesn't just prepare a home *for* us. He prepares His home *in* us.

We don't need to wait until heaven to feel at home in God's love. We can feel at home right now. We haven't been abandoned. As Jesus prepares an amazing future for us, He also prepares us for an amazing right now.

Lord, thank You for making Your home in my heart. Help me live for You today, even as You prepare an amazing future for me.

PRIORITY

"Seek the Kingdom of God above all else, and live righteously, and he will give you everything you need."
MATTHEW 6:33 NLT

Charles Mulli was six years old when he was abandoned by his mother and father. Homeless in Kenya, he was passed around to various relatives. At age sixteen, Charles was invited to a church youth rally, met Jesus, and found a new home in God's family.

Two years later, Charles found work doing odd jobs around Nairobi. This led to employment with better pay and the stirring of an entrepreneurial spirit. He bought a van, which he turned into a taxi. The venture blossomed into an entire transportation company called Mullyways, followed by other businesses in insurance and gas and automotive parts distribution.

Mulli's wealth grew beyond anything he could have imagined in his youth. But one day in 1986, exiting his Mercedes-Benz in Nairobi, he encountered a group of street children and was reminded of his homelessness as a youth.

It was then that Charles Mulli made a resolution: he was going to get these kids off the streets, no matter what it took, just as God had done for him years earlier.

Mulli sold his businesses and used the money to serve the children of Kenya. To date he has helped raise *twelve thousand* children, teaching them life skills and sharing the life-changing Gospel of Jesus.

Our own callings will likely look different than Charles Mulli's. But our priority should be the same: seeking the kingdom above all else, living righteously, and allowing God to provide for our needs.

Lord, You bless me in so many ways. Help me to make service to others—which is service to You—my priority.

SALVATION

"Salvation is found in no one else, for there is no other name under heaven given to mankind by which we must be saved."

ACTS 4:12 NIV

Just hours before Jesus allowed Himself to be arrested, tried, and crucified by the authorities of His day, He told His disciples, "I am the way and the truth and the life. No one comes to the Father except through me" (John 14:6).

Those are strong words, and they don't go over well in today's culture, which values diversity and inclusion above all other things. Simply put, the message of salvation through Jesus—and Jesus alone—is offensive in today's world.

Sadly, the world's thinking has had an effect on the way many Christians, especially younger ones, view sharing their faith. One recent poll of Christian millennials—people born between 1981 and 1996—showed that almost half believed that it is wrong to talk to others about salvation through Jesus.

Many belief systems and religions give people a sense of fulfillment, a moral compass, or a purpose in life. But there is only one way to come to God for salvation—and it's through Jesus. That's the message the Bible calls "the Gospel," and it's one of hope not condemnation. It's based on the one and only God reaching down to humanity and offering people a way to enjoy eternity in heaven with Him.

The Gospel of salvation through Jesus Christ is a great message. . .too great not to share with the people God puts in our lives.

Lord Jesus, thank You for coming to earth so that I could have eternal salvation through You. Please give me the courage and wisdom to point others toward You as the only door to the Father's throne room.

HONOR

Pray for us, for we are sure that we have a clear conscience, desiring to act honorably in all things.

HEBREWS 13:18 ESV

The Medal of Honor is the highest personal military decoration awarded by the United States of America. It's a recognition of valor and self-sacrifice.

Born in 1900, Henry Breault was the first submariner to receive the medal. Breault was in the torpedo room of U.S. submarine *0-5* when a collision with a steamship caused the sub to sink in less than a minute. Having climbed up to the hatch, Breault could see how quickly the ship was sinking. So he returned to the torpedo room to rescue a shipmate, sealing the hatch behind him. The two remained trapped together until they were rescued thirty-one hours later.

Not every honorable act will be as grand as saving another man's life. But every honorable act is worthwhile. To live with honor, we are called to live without regrets: we choose honesty over lying, purity over lust, and serving others over serving ourselves. It always comes down to the question "Who will I honor with my choices today?"

Being an honorable man doesn't happen by chance. It takes intention and prayer. We must make up our minds to do right and pray constantly for the Holy Spirit's assistance.

When we live an honorable life for God, we get far more than an earthly medal. God will give us the crown of life.

Lord, help me to be an honorable man. Whether I'm laying my life down or laying my preferences down, help me put others before myself and Your desires before all else. May I live a life without regrets, ready at all times to sacrifice for others like You did for me.

ACCEPTED

To the praise of the glory of his grace, wherein he hath made us accepted in the beloved.

EPHESIANS 1:6 KJV

Nineteen-year-old Daniel Sanchez was homeless and jobless when he met Fransonet "Jinji" Martinez—owner of Jinji Boxing Club in Lancaster, Pennsylvania. But Daniel had a knack for boxing, and he respected Martinez, who allowed him into his home. Jinji took the young man to church, helped him find a job, and pushed him to quit smoking marijuana. Sanchez even began referring to Martinez and his wife as Mom and Dad.

"All he did was help," Martinez told a Lancaster newspaper. "He did it because he wanted to be accepted. He wanted to be a son."

Sanchez's story made the news after he was killed in a shooting in 2017. Thankfully, he had found an earthly family who took him in and loved him before his tragic death.

Few of us have had as difficult a life as Daniel Sanchez.

But we've all made poor decisions that leave us feeling far from other people—and God. But "to the praise of the glory of his grace," He has made us accepted in Jesus Christ.

The Greek word translated "accepted" means "graced, endued with special honor, made to be highly favored." Just as Jinji Martinez accepted Daniel Sanchez into his home, making him part of his family, so God will accept all of us into His.

All we have to do is call on His name. God recognized that we could never live up to His standard of perfection, so He sent His only Son to die in our place as full payment for our sins. Accept that, and He accepts you.

Father, may I always be astounded by Your acceptance of me.

FREEDOM

Stand fast therefore in the liberty wherewith Christ hath made us free, and be not entangled again with the yoke of bondage.

GALATIANS 5:1 KJV

Ever hear this story?

A man came across a small traveling circus. As he passed the tents and trailers, he noticed a number of full-grown African elephants. But what he saw stopped him dead in his tracks: to the man's amazement, the massive creatures were being held in place by a small rope tied loosely around their front leg. No heavy chains. No iron bars. The elephants could easily break free from their ropes at any time. But for some reason they wouldn't.

The man asked the elephant handler why these powerful, intelligent animals made no attempt to escape. "When they are very young," the handler replied, "we use a small rope to bind them. At that age, it's more than enough to keep them in line. As they grow older, they slowly come to believe they cannot escape, so they never even *try* to break free."

Like those elephants, how many of us go through life chained to the belief that we are stuck—that we cannot do something simply because we have failed before? Worse, many times we're stuck simply because someone else told us we'd fail.

How about you? What are you chained to today? What yoke, seen or unseen, has stolen your freedom? What cost seems too great? What road seems too hard? Whatever it is, *the price has already been paid.* Freedom is yours. Slip off the rope and walk away. Jesus died to set you free.

Jesus, I thank You for the courage to step out of these chains and walk in freedom. You gave everything to make that possible!

PURE

Who shall ascend into the hill of the LORD? or who shall stand in his holy place? He that hath clean hands, and a pure heart.

PSALM 24:3–4 KJV

Billy Graham is remembered as one of the greatest evangelists of all time. For decades, he shared the message of Jesus' life, death, and resurrection with millions of people in countries around the globe. He also provided spiritual counsel to eleven U.S. presidents and numerous world leaders. But despite the temptations of fame, Billy Graham kept himself and his ministry pure.

In 1948, he and his staff developed the "Modesto Manifesto," four rules to help them remain above reproach as they traveled and ministered. The rules were (1) never be alone with a woman that is not your wife, (2) be financially accountable, (3) be honest, and (4) work with local churches, not against them. Billy Graham knew that he and his team represented Jesus, not just themselves, and they were proactive in their vigilance to protect the Lord's name.

Undoubtedly, they were very familiar with the verse that says, "Not many of you should become teachers, my fellow believers, because you know that we who teach will be judged more strictly" (James 3:1 NIV).

There is a spotlight on all who call themselves Christians. If we publicly profess our faith in Jesus, as He compels us to do in Matthew 10:32, we will be scrutinized—and rightly so. Will we take our commitment as seriously as Billy Graham did? Would you like to be as effective in life and fondly remembered in death as Billy Graham was? Keep your heart pure.

Father, I thank You for protecting me when I am tempted. I long to bring glory to Your name in everything I do.

FOCUS

Fixing our eyes on Jesus, the author and perfecter of faith, who for the joy set before Him endured the cross, despising the shame, and has sat down at the right hand of the throne of God.

HEBREWS 12:2 NASB

When we use the word *focus* as a verb, it indicates we are concentrating on something, directing all our attention at a target. In Hebrews 12:2, the apostle Paul gives us the target: Jesus. Each day, as we carry our own crosses (Luke 9:23), our focus should be fixed on Jesus, who set our example. And we should never give anything less than our absolute best. Like Hebrews 12:1 says, "Let us run with *endurance* the race that is set before us" (emphasis added).

In any race, the track is marked out with barriers and walls, and the finish line is predetermined. It's simply up to us to reach it. However, there's nothing simple about the race of our lives.

Life is not a "fun run" without hills or other challenges. Our contest is better compared to a Tough Mudder or a Spartan Race. Our spirits, emotions, and often our physical bodies will be tested. Satan will throw out any obstacle he can to distract our focus—much like he did with Job, attempting to make us deny God and forfeit our race.

But Job kept his focus, and we can too. If our gaze is fixed on the finish line—on Jesus—we will succeed. If we run with endurance, we will ultimately be with our Lord as an heir to the throne of God!

Heavenly Father, You have carried Your cross in order that I may too. Grant me the strength to endure this race that one day I may see You face-to-face. Amen.

BELIEF

But we ought always to thank God for you, brothers and sisters loved by the Lord, because God chose you as firstfruits to be saved through the sanctifying work of the Spirit and through belief in the truth.

2 THESSALONIANS 2:13 NIV

If you're a sports fan, you know how often *belief* can propel an athlete or team to great success.

During the 1973 season, frustrated New York Mets pitcher Tug McGraw met with a friend named Joe Badamo. McGraw told Badamo that he was giving up too many line drives, and his confidence was shaken. Badamo told his friend, "You got to believe." McGraw left the meeting with those words on his mind, ultimately tightening them to "Ya gotta believe." That became the Mets' slogan for 1973, and they went on to win the National League pennant.

At the 2009 United States Open tennis tournament, an unknown seventeen-year-old player put the word *believe* on her pink-and-yellow sneakers. Melanie Oudin's belief grew as she knocked off fourth-seeded Elena Dementieva, followed by a stunning win against 2006 champion Maria Sharapova. Her run ended in the fourth round, but she wouldn't have made it as far as she did without believing it was possible.

In today's passage, the apostle Paul links salvation to the sanctifying work of the Holy Spirit and "belief in the truth." This belief, in the truth as found in scripture, is stronger than any sports slogan. It's life-changing and eternity-altering.

How has believing the truth of God's Word shaped you in the past? How is it shaping you right now? Pinpoint one area of your life in which the Bible is challenging you, and act on that belief.

Father, thank You for saving me through the work of Your Spirit and through my belief in truth.

HEART

Above all else, guard your heart,
for everything you do flows from it.
PROVERBS 4:23 NIV

The heart tirelessly pumps gallons of blood, sending oxygen and nutrients through our bodies, from before we are born until the instant of death. But most of the time when "the heart" is mentioned in the Bible, it isn't referring to the muscle in our chest. The biblical heart is our core being, our emotions and minds.

When the author of Proverbs 4:23 tells us to guard our hearts, he isn't saying we should wear a bullet-proof vest. He's telling us to actively protect our core being. How? By managing our desires carefully and being diligent to think about the right things.

How can you know if you are guarding your heart well? Do a treasure check. Jesus says, "Where your treasure is, there your heart will be also" (Matthew 6:21). If your treasure is an earthly desire, your heart is vulnerable to attack. But if your desires are for God's glory in everything you do, your heart is more than bullet-proof—it's sin-proof.

When your heart is guarded, your desires are pure, and everything you do will be for the right reasons. If your treasure check revealed that you are valuing the wrong things, consciously and intentionally let them go. Grab on to God.

It's all for proper heart health.

Lord, keep my heart safe today. Hold on to it for me. May I treasure You above all else so that Your love and wisdom flow into every area of my life.

GIFTS

Every good and perfect gift is from above, coming down from the Father of the heavenly lights, who does not change like shifting shadows.

JAMES 1:17 NIV

Jaco Pastorius was a child prodigy. He revolutionized the way the bass guitar is played, redefining the sound of thc instrument for jazz players—and pretty much everyone else—forever. For many, he is the best and most influential bass guitarist the world has ever known.

In his book *Jaco: The Extraordinary and Tragic Life of Jaco Pastorius*, Bill Milkowski records a conversation between the musician, who was nearing his eighteenth birthday, and his younger brother, Rory. "Jaco looked me in the eye and said real seriously, 'Rory, man, I'm the best bass player on earth.' I looked back at him and said, 'I know.' "

At first glance that statement seems prideful, even arrogant. But here's the thing: Jaco really was the best of the best. Like every great musician, he had worked at his craft. But the extraordinary talent he possessed was his from day one. It was a gift.

It's important to remember that gifts *are given.* Those of us who are Christians understand that the gifts and talents we possess have been given to us by God. They are tangible expressions of His love, freely distributed to enrich our lives and make us a blessing to everyone around us. But it's up to us to use them.

"Use what talents you possess," the American clergyman and author Henry Van Dyke (1852–1933) once said. "The woods would be very silent if no birds sang there except those that sang best."

Jesus, I thank You for the gifts You've given me. Let me use them in a way that brings hope and joy to the people in my life.

COURAGE

"Have I not commanded you? Be strong and courageous. Do not be afraid; do not be discouraged, for the LORD your God will be with you wherever you go."

JOSHUA 1:9 NIV

Some might call it an act of courage for filmmaker Clint Eastwood to cast Spencer Stone, Alek Skarlatos, and Anthony Sadler as themselves in the film *The 15:17 to Paris*. But the director's decision was nothing compared to the three friends' exploits in foiling a 2015 terrorist attack.

When a gunman threatened their passenger train, the American buddies—two of them members of the military—sprang into action, subduing the terrorist and assisting a fellow passenger who had been shot in the scuffle. No doubt their military training had helped to prepare them for such a crisis situation.

We can hope we never need to wrestle a gun from a terrorist, but many other tough situations in life—marriage problems, difficulties at work, the crumbling of our personal ambitions—will catch us by surprise. How do we develop the courage we need to face such challenges head-on?

A military hero from the Bible offers insight. Joshua, the handpicked successor to Moses, got a strong dose of courage from God's presence: "Do not be afraid; do not be discouraged, for the LORD your God will be with you wherever you go" (Joshua 1:9).

That promise to Joshua is our promise too as it was basically repeated in the New Testament: "God has said, 'Never will I leave you; never will I forsake you.' So we say with confidence, 'The Lord is my helper; I will not be afraid. What can mere mortals do to me?' " (Hebrews 13:5–6).

True courage comes from our powerful, ever-present God.

Father, please remind me of Your presence today and every day.

OBEDIENCE

Be careful to obey all these regulations I am giving you, so that it may always go well with you and your children after you, because you will be doing what is good and right in the eyes of the L*ORD* *your God.*

DEUTERONOMY 12:28 NIV

Even if you're not into poetry, you may be familiar with Alfred, Lord Tennyson's "The Charge of the Light Brigade." Key lines include, "Theirs not to make reply, / Theirs not to reason why, / Theirs but to do and die. / Into the valley of Death / Rode the six hundred."

The poem commemorates heroic British soldiers in the Crimean War. The Light Brigade received orders to storm a heavily defended Russian position during the 1854 battle of Balaklava. Though they were fully aware of their enemy's strength, the six hundred men, armed with spears and lances, obeyed and charged. Over half were killed, wounded, or captured.

The Light Brigade is a noble example of obedience, but Jesus Christ is the ultimate. "Being in very nature

God," the apostle Paul writes, "he humbled himself by becoming obedient to death—even death on a cross!" (Philippians 2:6, 8).

We are called to the same kind of obedience, at least figuratively. In the Bible, we read commands to be faithful to our wives, to love our neighbors as ourselves, to place nothing before God. Some of these seem easy enough, but challenges arise every day. Even so, God calls us to be obedient—and He offers an incredible reward. Remember that Jesus, who "learned obedience from what he suffered. . .became the source of eternal salvation for all who obey him" (Hebrews 5:8–9).

Lord, help me surrender all areas of my life to You. May I always remember my duty is to obey.

ZEALOUS

Who gave himself for us to redeem us from all lawlessness and to purify for himself a people for his own possession who are zealous for good works.

TITUS 2:14 ESV

A zealot is a person who takes on a cause. Often, the two become synonymous.

Guys of a certain age might remember the zeal of businessman Victor Kiam II. Though he worked for several companies and subsequently owned a number of businesses, he is best known for his purchase of Remington Products. Kiam acquired the company in 1979, not long after his wife had given him a Remington electric shaver as a gift. In advertisements throughout the United States and the United Kingdom, Kiam served as his own company's pitchman and became a household name in the 1980s. Remember his tagline? "I liked the shaver so much, I bought the company." That's being zealous!

The apostle Paul was an even more zealous presenter of the infinitely more important "product" that he'd discovered: the Gospel of Jesus Christ. And Paul's letter to Titus encouraged his younger colleague to be that same type of individual. Paul reminded Titus that followers of Jesus Christ need to be "zealous for good works"—the type of actions that advance the cause of Christ and bless those who have been redeemed.

If a businessman can be remembered for his electric shaver commercials decades after they aired, can't we as God's redeemed people be known for our good works? Today, think of a kindness you can perform in the name of Christ—and do it with zeal.

Father, please help me remember who I am in Christ and the mission I've been given–to be zealous for good works.

RICHES

Oh, the depth of the riches of the wisdom and knowledge of God! How unsearchable his judgments, and his paths beyond tracing out!

ROMANS 11:33 NIV

In Matthew 19:16–22, we meet a wealthy young man who allowed his earthly riches to keep him from following Jesus. After hearing this man claim he had kept the whole law since his youth, Jesus told him, "If you want to be perfect, go, sell your possessions and give to the poor, and you will have treasure in heaven. Then come, follow me" (verse 21).

What happened next was truly heartbreaking. Instead of doing as Jesus had said, the man walked away. He wasn't willing to let go of his possessions and prestige.

While He was on earth, Jesus taught His followers an important truth about earthly riches: "Do not store up for yourselves treasures on earth, where moths and vermin destroy, and where thieves break in and steal. But store up for yourselves treasures in heaven, where moths and vermin do not destroy, and where thieves do not break in and steal" (Matthew 6:19–20).

We receive true, everlasting riches when we know God in a personal, loving way—when we seek Him in all things and follow Him wherever He leads. These are the riches that no one can take from us, the kind that never wear out or lose their value. They're riches God freely gives to those so focused on Jesus that nothing can steal away their affection.

Generous heavenly Father, as I work hard to make my way in this world, remind me daily that my focus should be on the everlasting riches You give—the eternal treasures You have for those who love You and put You first in everything.

TRUST

Trust in the LORD with all your heart and lean not on your own understanding.

PROVERBS 3:5 NIV

People put their trust in a lot of things. They *trust* that their cars will start, move, and stop when they need them to. And when they board a commercial airliner, people *trust* in the plane's soundness and the pilot's knowledge.

These are good but imperfect illustrations of what the word *trust* means. Even the best-built cars sometimes break down, and commercial flights do, on very rare occasions, end in terrible accidents. Yet we still put our trust in them. What else are we supposed to do?

The Bible tells us we can completely trust God, knowing that He never fails or makes mistakes. He always does what is best for those who love and follow Him. We can trust God with everything in us, even when our circumstances tell us to worry and fret and try to make things better on our own.

That's the kind of God we serve. The kind of God

who loves us more than we can ever understand. The kind of God who has proven Himself over and over to be worthy of our love, our devotion. . .and our trust.

Few things in this world are worthy of absolute trust. But we can unreservedly trust our Father in heaven in all things. He knows what He's doing, and He's big and mighty enough to handle even our toughest problems.

Father in heaven, You are in control of all things, including everything that happens in my life. I am amazed that You are so big–that You created such a vast universe–yet You care so much about someone as small as me. Thank You, Lord.

CALM

He maketh the storm a calm.

Psalm 107:29 KJV

Have you ever been at the water's edge after a storm? If so, you'll recall the smooth surface of the lake or pond and perhaps the soothing calls of birds in the distance. Maybe you have wondered why you don't make time to enjoy such experiences more often. Life can be crazy, and we yearn for periods of calm like this.

Psalm 107 paints a picture of mariners and fisherman on the sea (verses 23–24), men who know that God is in control of the wind and rain: "For he commandeth, and raiseth the stormy wind, which lifteth up the waves thereof" (verse 25). When those storms arise, the seafarers cry out to the Lord for deliverance (verse 28). God answers, and "maketh the storm a calm" (verse 29).

In Matthew 8:23–27, we read about Jesus doing the same thing. His power caused the disciples to ask, "What manner of man is this, that even the winds and the sea obey him!" (verse 27). We know the answer: Jesus is the

Messiah, God in the flesh, the creator of the heavens and earth (John 1:3, Colossians 1:16–17), and He has no trouble calming a storm with just a simple command or gesture.

In each of these passages, people facing a storm cried out to the Lord—and He heard their cry. What sort of "storm" are you facing right now at work, at home, at church, or in your own body? Are you filled with anxiety? Cry out to the Lord. Nothing is beyond His control.

Father, I'm quicker to complain about storms than I am to cry out to You in them. My soul longs for a sense of calmness. Please deliver me, O Lord.

SEPARATION

Neither height nor depth, nor anything else in all creation, will be able to separate us from the love of God that is in Christ Jesus our Lord.

ROMANS 8:39 NIV

Some guys enjoy being alone, but no one has known the kind of solitude Michael Collins experienced in July 1969.

He was part of Apollo 11, the U.S. space mission that first landed men on the moon. Collins stayed in the orbiting command module *Columbia* while his fellow astronauts descended to the surface in the lunar module *Eagle*. Neil Armstrong and "Buzz" Aldrin walked on the barren, airless surface 240,000 miles from earth, but at least they were together. In the command module, Collins was absolutely alone—even more so when *Columbia*'s path carried it around the far side of the moon, beyond even radio contact with anyone else.

Collins recorded his thoughts as he awaited the other astronauts' return, which was anything but guaranteed.

"If a count were taken," he said from the abyss of space, "the score would be three billion plus two over on the other side of the moon, and one plus God-knows-what on this side."

The former test pilot said later that he felt "anticipation, satisfaction, [and] confidence" more than loneliness. But most of us experience loneliness at some time or another, even when we're among people. That's a sad fact of humanity's fall, which separated us from God and each other.

Happily, God enacted a plan to bridge the abyss—sending Jesus to die on the cross for our sins. And when we accept that solution by faith, we are permanently connected to Him. Nothing in all creation—even the massive bulk of the moon—could separate us from God's love.

Father, You and I are inseparable.
Thank You for Your love.

COMPASSION

Finally, all of you, be like-minded, be sympathetic, love one another, be compassionate and humble.

1 PETER 3:8 NIV

During a preseason football game between the Oakland Raiders and Seattle Seahawks in September 2018, eight-year-old Donovan Shaw spotted a fellow youngster who seemed to be lost. Stadium staff tried to help until the boy's father arrived, but Donovan recognized his sadness and decided to do something.

Donovan left his own group, walked down to the boy, and said they could watch the game together until his father arrived. The two immediately became buddies, and the story came to light when a nearby fan, Chelsea Burke, snapped a photo of Donovan with his arm around the boy. Touched by this act of compassion, she posted the picture on social media, where many others were similarly moved.

When a reporter asked Donovan about his kind gesture, the eight-year-old answered, "I saw him and just felt sorry for him. So I asked him to sit down because I wanted him to feel better."

Even cold hearts can be warmed when they see compassion in action. And this is a tremendous opportunity for us as Christians. Today, keep your eyes open for opportunities to show compassion to others—even if they don't deserve it. Maybe *especially* if they don't deserve it.

The apostle Peter wrote his first letter to Christians "scattered throughout the provinces of Pontus, Galatia, Cappadocia, Asia, and Bithynia" (1 Peter 1:1). With that in mind, how might you show compassion to people from other towns, states, or even nations?

Father, compassion is a simple way that I can model Christ's love for others. Show me opportunities today that will make a lasting impact for Your kingdom.

THINKING

For as he thinks within himself, so he is.

PROVERBS 23:7 NASB

Imagine that each morning, at breakfast time, you are offered two pills. One will give you whatever desires you have for the day. The other will take you on a spiritual journey. Trying to take both, though, will cancel them both out. You must choose one or the other.

In Galatians 5:16–17 (NIV,) the apostle Paul wrote, "So I say, walk by the Spirit, and you will not gratify the desires of the flesh. For the flesh desires what is contrary to the Spirit, and the Spirit what is contrary to the flesh. They are in conflict with each other, so that you are not to do whatever you want."

What does Galatians 5:16–17 have to do with Proverbs 23:7? Well, which pill do you choose to take each morning? Is it the spiritual pill? Or perhaps the one that sounds a little more enticing? The pill we choose determines the way we think—and the way we think determines the pill we choose.

To make this a little more personal, let's look at it this way: As I think within myself, I am. Am I thinking through God's Spirit? Or through my flesh?

Father, I pray that my thoughts would be upright and pure and that each morning I would choose to walk with You. I commit to thinking through Your Spirit rather than my flesh from the moment I wake up each day. Amen.

TRUTH

"Then you will know the truth,
and the truth will set you free."
JOHN 8:32 NIV

In the 2013 film *12 Years a Slave*, a Canadian laborer named Samuel Bass confronts the cruel Southern slaveholder Edwin Epps. Epps defends himself by saying he hasn't done anything against the law. But Bass answers, "Laws change, Epps. Universal truths are constant. It is a fact, a plain and simple fact, that what is true and right is true and right for all."

That's not a popular way of thinking today. The modern world argues that each person must develop his own standards for right and wrong. But Bass's statement is a pretty good reflection of the Bible's teaching.

Society's laws do change, as do worldly moral standards and human ways of thinking. But truth—God's truth as He has recorded it in His written Word—has never changed and never will change. What is right in God's eyes has always been and always will be right.

What is wrong in His eyes has always been and will always be wrong.

Many believe that following absolute standards of truth limits people. In some ways that is true: when we live according to biblical teachings, we can't do just anything we want. But God has arranged the world in such a way that knowing and following truth actually sets people free—free to know Him deeply, free to be better people, free to serve and love others more effectively.

God's truth, then, doesn't limit us as Christians. On the contrary, it's true freedom.

God of truth, what this world calls "truth" seems to change daily. Help me to remain focused on and committed to Your truth in every area of my life.

CELEBRATE

"But we had to celebrate and rejoice, for this brother of yours was dead and has begun to live, and was lost and has been found."

LUKE 15:32 NASB

In 2018, the world tuned in to hope and pray for the rescue of twelve boys and their twenty-five-year-old soccer coach who had become trapped in a cave in Thailand. One of the players, Pheeraphat Sompiengjai, was supposed to celebrate his sixteenth birthday the day the group went exploring underground and found themselves cut off by floodwaters.

As various rescue efforts were begun, discarded, and modified, Sompiengjai's family never gave up hope. They had a birthday cake waiting for him in the refrigerator, so imagine the celebration when he finally emerged from the cave after two full weeks.

If a father believes he's lost his child but then catches a distant glimpse of the boy returning home, how could he do anything other than celebrate? That's exactly the scene depicted in today's verse from Jesus' parable of the lost (or prodigal) son. He'd been trapped in a cave of wild living before coming to his senses and returning home. In this story, the father represents God, who celebrates every time one of His children turns from sin and returns to the fold.

Do you have some entangling sin that you've grown tired of indulging? Have you seen the error of your ways? It's never too late to return home. Leave that old life behind and run toward the Father. He'll be waiting with open arms. Maybe even a celebratory cake.

Father, sometimes after seasons of sin I have feared returning to You, not certain of how You would respond. Forgive me, Lord, for not realizing that You would celebrate.

FRIENDSHIP

"I no longer call you servants, because a servant does not know his master's business. Instead, I have called you friends, for everything that I learned from my Father I have made known to you."

JOHN 15:15 NIV

Love him or hate him, Bob Dylan is an American icon. And his 1979 song "Gotta Serve Somebody" makes a profound statement. From the very first line, Dylan gets right to the point: he prods his listeners to remember that whoever we are and whatever we do, we're gonna have to serve somebody. Every one of us—doctor, lawyer, Indian chief, businessman, preacher, or some high-level thief—spends at least some part of each day in service to someone else. And there's certainly nothing wrong with that.

Earning status as a well-respected servant can be appealing, especially to our flesh. After all, service can be measured, quantified, lauded, and rewarded. But Jesus said, "A servant does not know his master's business."

Instead, He has called us "friends." Friendship can be trickier than servanthood because it says a lot about *who we are* without giving much thought—sometimes none at all—to *what we do*.

So how does Jesus see us? Are we servants only, whose primary value lies in our willingness or ability to perform tasks according to instruction, without question or resistance? Or does He see us as His much-loved children? Does He view us as His *friends*? John 15:15 is pretty clear.

To find someone in this world who knows pretty much everything about you and still likes you is amazing if not downright unbelievable. Jesus definitely knows everything about you, and what does He say? "I have called you friends."

Lord, thank You so much for calling me "friend." What more could I ask for?

UNIQUE

I praise you; for I am fearfully and wonderfully made. Wonderful are your works; my soul knows it very well.

PSALM 139:14 ESV

Advertising has become an ever-present part of our daily experience. Computer algorithms crunch data from our phones, our credit cards, and our web searches and send back a barrage of information about the latest and greatest products and services. A significant part of every ad campaign is "distinction": Why is product A better than product B or company Y more competent or trustworthy than company Z? If advertising promotes something without presenting it as distinct or unique, it's not being done correctly.

Certainly, these notions of uniqueness and distinction apply to every human being—all seven billion of us. Each and every one of us were created "fearfully and wonderfully" by almighty God. No one else, whether now, in the past, or in the future, combines all the elements that make you *you*. Only you live where you live, work where you work, like what you like, and do what you do. Your interests and peculiarities are yours alone. Add in your personal experiences and your willingness to serve the Lord, and you can begin to understand the beauty of God's special act of creation when He made you. Sure, we all share characteristics with other people—maybe even a lot of other people—but each one of us is blessed with our own unique gifts and abilities, perspectives and solutions.

In a world of untold choices and challenges, God needs you—wonderful, unique you—to advertise His honor and glory to others. Be unique—uniquely you, uniquely His.

Lord, help me to know the blessing of being fearfully and wonderfully made. I praise You for Your wonderful works.

PRAISE

Let everything that has breath
praise the Lord. Praise the Lord.
PSALM 150:6 NIV

If you're reading this, you have breath—so your job is to praise the Lord. That seems easier at some times than others. It would seem impossible in seasons of depression or the unfathomable hardships that Horatio Spafford faced.

If you're not familiar with his name, you may recognize his hymn, "It Is Well with My Soul." One stanza repeats the phrase "Praise the Lord," and you might think the song was written during a high point in Spafford's life. You would be wrong.

Horatio Spafford knew tragedy and deep heartache. He had lost a young son to illness and much of his business was destroyed in the Great Chicago Fire of 1871. Two years later, having recovered financially, he planned a family holiday to Europe. Detained at the last minute by business, Spafford sent his wife and four daughters ahead—but during the voyage, their ship struck another vessel and his four daughters perished.

Crossing the ocean to reunite with his wife, Spafford wrestled with his pain and loss. But he ultimately penned a song that begins, "When peace like a river attendeth my way. . ."

In Psalm 34:1 David writes, "I will extol the LORD at all times; his praise will always be on my lips." This man, who like Horatio Spafford faced many painful life experiences, did not put a condition on when to praise God. He simply *chose* to do so.

And so should we. Consider the very breath in your lungs and use it to praise the Lord.

Lord, I choose to use the breath You have given me to praise You. Through my testimony, may others be drawn to Your goodness.

VIRTUE

Finally, brethren, whatsoever things are true, whatsoever things are honest, whatsoever things are just, whatsoever things are pure, whatsoever things are lovely, whatsoever things are of good report; if there be any virtue, and if there be any praise, think on these things.

PHILIPPIANS 4:8 KJV

The great track and field athlete Jesse Owens, who won four gold medals at the 1936 Olympic Games in Munich, Germany, knew the importance of disciplining his mind and body. To become perhaps the greatest track star in American history, he'd had to learn those things.

"The battles that count aren't the ones for gold medals," he once said. "The struggles within yourself, the invisible, inevitable battles inside us all, that's where it's at."

The Bible says a lot about the battles that go on inside every believer, and in Philippians 4:8, the apostle Paul advises us to engage in what we could call "virtuous thinking." That means thinking on things that have virtue, a word meaning "excellence" or "goodness."

It's not easy to avoid bad thoughts. Just try this experiment: if you say, "I'm not going to think about elephants," your mind almost immediately goes to a huge gray animal with a long trunk and floppy ears. Paul suggests a more positive way to train our minds: choosing to focus on those things that God says have virtue, things that will grow us in our faith.

This will take work, not unlike the rigorous training of an Olympic champion. But with the right mix of Bible truth and the Holy Spirit's power, we can do it.

Think on these things.

Righteous, loving God, help me to focus my mind on the things that please You. Help me to grow in virtue in my relationship with Jesus Christ.

BLESSINGS

The godly are showered with blessings.
PROVERBS 10:6 NLT

When the Lord called Abram (Genesis 12:1–3), He promised to make Abram a blessing to the whole world. God said that all the families on earth would be blessed through this one man—meaning others would prosper as a result of his answering the call to leave the country of his birth. This was God's covenant with Abram.

God would multiply Abram's offspring as the stars of the heavens and the sand of the seashore—and eventually provide the ultimate blessing, Jesus Christ, through Abram's family line. But God didn't stop there. As you answer the call to join His family, He promises to shower *you* with blessings as well.

These blessings will look different from one believer to the next. They may include material prosperity, such as possessions or wealth. They may include physical health, friends, and family. Or they might not.

But God's blessings definitely include spiritual

benefits. The apostle Paul picked up this theme in Ephesians 1:6, where he said, "We praise God for the glorious grace he has poured out on us who belong to his dear Son." In other words, God has made us acceptable in His sight through Jesus Christ. What better blessing could we ask for?

While the blessings of this life are necessarily limited in duration, the spiritual benefits we get from knowing Jesus continue through all eternity. As the psalmist David put it, "You will show me the way of life, granting me the joy of your presence and the pleasures of living with you forever" (Psalm 16:11).

Father, I often take my blessings from You for granted. The next time I do, please remind me of the riches of Your grace.

GLORY

O Lord, our Lord, how excellent is thy name in all the earth! who hast set thy glory above the heavens.

PSALM 8:1 KJV

The heavens declare the *glory* of God.

When was the last time you stopped and really looked up at the night sky? The reality of infinity and the sheer beauty of creation can be overwhelming, to say the least.

Most galaxies contain at least a trillion stars. Our galaxy, the Milky Way, contains about 250 billion stars, making it pretty average as galaxies go. The Andromeda Galaxy, which can be seen with the naked eye, is about 2,538,000 light-years away. That means if you got in your car right now and drove at the speed of light (which you probably do most of the time anyway), it would take about 2.54 million years to get there—not counting bathroom breaks and stops at Starbucks.

Is it possible that we have become so distracted by the noise of our own lives that we've forgotten who God—who Jesus Christ—really is? Yes, we love Him.

Yes, we love His Word. We are thankful for all the good things He has given us. But have we forgotten that we exist because He decided to create us? That we have a place to exist because He made that too?

What do you make? Maybe some coffee. A piece of art. Maybe even a house. God makes galaxies. There's quite a bit of difference between what we make and who we are. That difference is the glory of God.

Saint Irenaeus said the glory of God is man fully alive. Are you fully alive today?

Thank You, Jesus, for giving me life. Let me never take for granted the magnitude of all You've done to make me fully alive.

HUMILITY

Humble yourselves in the sight of the Lord, and he shall lift you up.

JAMES 4:10 KJV

Bear Bryant, the legendary football coach at the University of Alabama, is quoted as saying, "If you believe in yourself and have dedication and pride and never quit, you'll be a winner. The price of victory is high, but so are the rewards."

Sounds great, doesn't it? Society has always encouraged men to be winners, to work hard and take pride in their accomplishments. So when the Bible tells us to *humble* ourselves, we men don't always know what to do with that. Humility is for the losers, not the winners, right?

It is good to work hard and do things well. But Christians should be wary of taking pride in their accomplishments. As C. S. Lewis said in his book *Mere Christianity*, "A proud man is always looking down on things and people; and, of course, as long as you are looking down, you cannot see something that is above you."

The trouble for men isn't the desire for success—it's how we go about it. When we spend our energy trying to look good to others, our reward is temporary. But when we live a life of humility before God, doing what He wants us to do, He will lift us up in ways that we can't even begin to imagine.

The price of that victory is even higher than hard work. It is humility in a world that encourages pride.

Lord, when I feel like drawing attention to myself and my accomplishments, help me to be humble before You. May I never judge my success by what others think, when Your opinion is the only one that matters.

LISTENING

"Give ear and come to me; listen, that you may live. I will make an everlasting covenant with you, my faithful love promised to David."

ISAIAH 55:3 NIV

Imagine for a moment that you have been given free tickets to a symphony that sold out months ago. On the night of the event, you settle into your seat and listen to the world-class musicians tuning their instruments. Then, just as the conductor brings down her baton to begin the performance, you pull out your phone to call your brother. Hey, it's been a while since you've talked.

Wait, what? That would never happen, right? Or if it did, it wouldn't be long until you were ushered out of the symphony.

The Austrian musician Alfred Brendel, known for his piano performances of the great composers, has pointed out that the word *listen* contains the same letters as the word *silent*.

That's a good point for us as Christians to remember.

We have been given free tickets to the greatest experience ever: a relationship with God. But how many times have we ignored Him or talked over Him because we had our own, seemingly more pressing concerns? We cannot listen to God if we are not silent before Him.

Ask God to quiet your heart and the noise of life around you. Then open the Bible and start reading. God has already spoken His truth to us. We can enjoy a harmonious relationship with Him if we simply start listening.

Lord, may I be silent before You. Help me to listen to those things that You have for me. Keep me from getting distracted or adding to the noise around me. Thank You for giving me the Bible so I can better hear Your truth.

ANGELS

Do not neglect to show hospitality to strangers, for thereby some have entertained angels unawares.

HEBREWS 13:2 ESV

At the time the letter to the Hebrews was written, public inns were not common. According to biblical scholar Adam Clarke (1760–1832), "It was an office of charity and mercy to receive, lodge, and entertain travelers; and this is what the apostle particularly recommends." In showing hospitality to strangers, some who originally read this epistle had actually entertained *angels* without even knowing it.

Scripture often commands God's people to welcome strangers (see, for example, Leviticus 19:34, 25:35–38; Deuteronomy 10:18-19; 1 Kings 17:10–16; Jeremiah 22:3; Matthew 25:35; and Titus 1:8) In Hebrews 13, the writer connects our hospitality to the notion that we may very well be serving angels. Why is that important?

Recall that Jesus once told a parable that indicated

meeting a stranger's temporal needs was actually a service to Him (Matthew 25:35–40). So whether we are entertaining fellow humans or "angels unawares," our acts of kindness are always done to the Lord.

Most of us want to be hospitable to strangers, but we aren't always sure how. Here are some simple, practical ideas: If you see a young mother digging through her purse at McDonald's—an obvious attempt to find enough money to pay for her children's meals—that's a perfect time to cover the bill. If you hear about a neighbor who was recently widowed or laid up by a surgery, offer to mow grass or shovel snow or buy groceries.

When we extend such simple kindnesses, we serve the Lord. . .and maybe even entertain angels.

Father, give me an opportunity today to meet a stranger's need. Give me eyes to see and the courage to help.

GRATITUDE

Enter into his gates with thanksgiving, and into his courts with praise: be thankful unto him, and bless his name.

PSALM 100:4 KJV

What are you thankful for today?

If there's one simple thing anyone can do to make everything better, it's being thankful. Nothing sweeps away the darkness and lets the sunshine in like a thankful heart.

This anonymous quote appeared online: "Some people could be given an entire field of roses and only see the thorns. Others could be given a single weed and only see a beautiful wildflower. Perception is the key component to gratitude. And gratitude is the key component to joy."

What if you actually had everything you ever wanted in your possession right this very minute? What would you do? How would you feel? More importantly, is it possible you actually *do* have everything but have become so distracted by the cares of this world that you can't even see God's goodness anymore?

"In every thing give thanks" (1 Thessalonians 5:18).

There is always something to be thankful for. When you can begin to thank God for everything—*everything*—the dark clouds that have surrounded your heart and mind will begin to melt away. Don't let the enemy rob you of one of the greatest gifts Jesus has to offer: your happiness.

This day can be filled with joy. Find something to thank God for today. Then do it again tomorrow—and the next day, and the day after that.

Jesus loves you. He is the everything you're looking for—the everything nothing can ever take away.

Jesus, I thank You for this beautiful day and all of the good things in it. Every good thing I have comes from You.

YIELDING

Neither yield ye your members as instruments of unrighteousness unto sin: but yield yourselves unto God, as those that are alive from the dead, and your members as instruments of righteousness unto God.

ROMANS 6:13 KJV

Modern versions of the Bible don't use the word *yield.* They translate the first part of Romans 6:13 as "Do not let any part of your body become an instrument of evil to serve sin" (NLT) or "Do not offer any part of yourself to sin as an instrument of wickedness" (NIV). *Yield* is a complex word with multiple definitions in the dictionary. Two in particular apply to this verse: to give oneself up to a habit or temptation, and to submit oneself to another.

Students are expected to submit to their teachers. Players need to submit to their coaches. Residents of cities, states, or nations must be prepared to obey their government's laws and regulations. You yield to these authorities, or you face the consequences—a trip to the principal's office, time on the bench, fines or even a prison sentence.

But there can be even heavier consequences to yielding to bad habits, temptations, and other sinful impulses. Every Christian has a choice each day: whether to yield to those negative influences or to God. His way may not always seem like the easy or "fun" way—but it's invariably the best way.

The Word of God is where we'll find His expectations and, often, even His reasons for them. Today, do you need to make the time to find out, from scripture, how to "yield yourselves unto God. . .and your members as instruments of righteousness"?

Father, show me the path of righteousness so I may yield to Your authority.

FILLING

May the God of hope fill you with all joy and peace as you trust in him, so that you may overflow with hope by the power of the Holy Spirit.

ROMANS 15:13 NIV

Fans of the venerable Twinkie were aghast in 2012 when the Hostess company declared bankruptcy—and declared that the sweet treat would no longer be made.

For eight decades, Twinkies had been a mainstay in the United States. Their popularity grew in the 1950s, when they sponsored *Howdy Doody*, a pioneer of children's television. But the junk food wasn't solely for kids—generations of adults enjoyed Twinkies as well. To many, the pleasure was in the crème filling, originally banana flavored but switched to vanilla during World War II due to fruit rationing.

So is it a stretch to compare Twinkie filling to the "filling" of joy and peace we get as we trust in God? Well, consider that both are sweet and satisfying. Both fill an empty space—the hollow core of a sponge cake and the hollow core of our human emotions. Without their respective "fillings," neither Twinkies nor humans are complete.

God's joy and peace, among the "fruit of the Spirit" (Galatians 5:22–23), are part of the hope He also provides. In fact, "everything we need for a godly life" comes through "our *knowledge* of him who called us" (2 Peter 1:3, emphasis added). The more we know God through His Word, the more we'll trust Him. The more we trust Him, the more joy and peace we'll experience. And then, according to Romans 15:13, our hope will overflow to others.

Good news: Twinkies are still around. And God still wants to fill *you* with joy, peace, and hope.

Lord, Your joy and peace are sweet. Satisfy me with Your hope.

HEAVEN

"What blessings await you when people hate you and exclude you and mock you and curse you as evil because you follow the Son of Man. When that happens, be happy! Yes, leap for joy! For a great reward awaits you in heaven. And remember, their ancestors treated the ancient prophets that same way."

LUKE 6:22–23 NLT

Think about your favorite movie. The first time you watched it, you were probably on the edge of your seat. You may have had a guess as to what would happen, but you didn't know for sure. The second time you watched it, you had a very different experience. You knew that everything would work out in the end, even while the main character was suffering in the middle.

In Luke 6:22–23, Jesus told His disciples that even though they might suffer for their faith on earth, "a great reward awaits you in heaven." No matter what the heavenly reward is, the very fact that we get one is more than we deserve.

How can we leap for joy when we face suffering? "We do this by keeping our eyes on Jesus, the champion who initiates and perfects our faith. Because of the joy awaiting him, he endured the cross, disregarding its shame. Now he is seated in the place of honor beside God's throne" (Hebrews 12:2).

Jesus knows our movie completely, and (spoiler alert) it ends in a great reward for the people who love Him. When things look dark, keep going. You can even leap for joy, confident that God has a plan that ends in the best way possible.

Lord, give me joy in my suffering. Help me focus on my heavenly rewards when my earthly experience is hard. Thank You for giving my movie a great ending.

CONTENTMENT

Yet true godliness with contentment
is itself great wealth.
1 TIMOTHY 6:6 NLT

John Newton had a way of putting the essentials of faith to verse. The slave-trader-turned-Anglican-clergyman penned several hymns that have stood the test of time, including one of the most beloved, "Amazing Grace."

One of Newton's lesser-known (and, by today's standards, oddly titled) hymns describes life without Jesus. The first stanza of "How Tedious and Tasteless" reads, "How tedious and tasteless the hours, / When Jesus no longer I see: / Sweet prospects, sweet birds, and sweet flowers, / Have all lost their sweetness to me; / The midsummer sun shines but dim, / The fields strive in vain to look gay; / But when I am happy in Him, / December's as pleasant as May."

Newton had a firm grasp on the truth of 1 Timothy 6:6: that true godliness with contentment is great wealth. Many of us have spent years seeking contentment in money, power, lust, and any number of other pursuits. But many of us have also learned (or will learn) that we'll never find contentment in such things.

Jesus told us exactly where to discover the contentment our souls crave: in Him. "Take my yoke upon you," He said. "Let me teach you, because I am humble and gentle at heart, and you will find rest for your souls" (Matthew 11:29).

It's time to put off the things of this world, what scripture calls "a craving for physical pleasure, a craving for everything we see, and pride in our achievements and possessions" (1 John 2:16). Contentment in Jesus is itself great wealth.

Father, I've often found fulfillment to be elusive—I realize now that I was seeking it in the wrong place. May I find my contentment only in You.

PERFECT

As for God, His way is perfect. The Word of the Lord has stood the test. He is a covering for all who go to Him for a safe place.

PSALM 18:30 NLV

David knew he was in trouble when Saul, the king of Israel, hurled a spear at him. God had given David success in everything he did, including his victory over the Philistine giant Goliath, which only fueled Saul's jealousy. David ran for his life, stopping in many places—including Gath, Goliath's birthplace—for refuge.

When the king of Gath grew suspicious, David put on a convincing display of insanity and soon was on the run again. Certainly, this was not the future David had envisioned when the aged prophet Samuel anointed him as the next king of Israel.

David ended up in a cave in the wilderness, where "all those who were in distress or in debt or discontented gathered around him, and he became their commander. About four hundred men were with him" (1 Samuel

22:2 NIV). The path to becoming the most celebrated king in Israel's history began in an overgrown hideout, surrounded by people who'd been discarded by society. Who could have known?

Well, God. His way is perfect.

Each of us arrives at many critical points in life, some we've aimed for (like a job promotion) and some we hope never to experience (like a sudden job loss). We may not know what God intends to do in these circumstances, but as followers of Jesus, we can be sure that His perfect way is unfolding to our benefit.

Even if that involves our removal to heaven. What could be more perfect than that?

Lord, I pray for faithfulness and patience as You work out Your perfect plan in me.

WONDER

*I will remember the works of the LORD:
surely I will remember thy wonders of old.*
PSALM 77:11 KJV

There's something about remembering good things from the past that can really bind friends and family together. It's always fun to break out the photo albums and old videos and then laugh, cry, and poke fun at one another—even exchange words of gratitude.

It's a lot like that in our relationship with God too.

Yes, the Bible warns us against dwelling too much in the past. But it also says that remembering the works and wonders of God is a good thing. When we do, we can thank Him for all that He's done.

That King James Version word *wonders* in Psalm 77:11 is rendered "wonderful deeds" in a modern translation. Throughout the Bible, and especially in the Old Testament, God told His people to remember the wonders He had performed for them and to pass those memories along to future generations. King David, who enjoyed many blessings from the hand of God, put it this way: "Let all that I am praise the LORD; may I never forget the good things he does for me" (Psalm 103:2 NLT).

So take some time to remember the wonders God has done for you. And make sure you never forget His greatest wonder of all—saving you, filling you with His Holy Spirit, and sending you on a new path. It's a path that leads to an eternity in heaven with Him.

Isn't that wonderful?

Gracious Father, I thank You for being so generous and gracious in Your blessings. Forgive me for when I forget those "wonders." Please help me to remember everything You do for me and to give You thanks.

PRESERVATION

He guards the course of the just and protects the way of his faithful ones.

PROVERBS 2:8 NIV

As a devout Seventh Day Adventist, Desmond Doss was a pacifist. Still, with World War II raging, he felt called to serve his country. Doss enlisted, hoping to become a medic. He was assigned to a rifle company.

You can imagine how a conscientious objector, a man who refused to carry a gun, was received by fellow recruits and the officer corps. But Desmond was undeterred, kindly and quietly working his way into a medic's role. Soon, he deployed to Okinawa.

There, Doss's unit was charged with scaling a cliff called the Maeda Escarpment, which troops nicknamed Hacksaw Ridge. Once his unit arrived atop, Japanese soldiers staged a vicious counterattack. U.S. officers called for a retreat, and the uninjured soldiers fell back immediately. One medic, though, returned to the battlefield over and over, rescuing more than seventy wounded soldiers all by himself.

The story of Desmond Doss is remarkable—how an unarmed, pacifist medic could be preserved from death in the wild firefights of Okinawa. You can chalk it up to luck, or you can see God's hand in it.

If we look at our own lives, though they're probably much less dramatic, we can undoubtedly recall moments when God preserved us too. As the psalmist David wrote, "Though I walk in the midst of trouble, you preserve my life. You stretch out your hand against the anger of my foes; with your right hand you save me" (Psalm 138:7).

Even when we lose our lives, we as Christians are preserved—if we are "away from the body," we are "at home with the Lord" (2 Corinthians 5:8). We really can't lose!

Lord, I praise You for continuously preserving my life.

VICTORY

But thanks be to God! He gives us the victory through our Lord Jesus Christ.
1 CORINTHIANS 15:57 NIV

It's safe to say that most guys like to win. Whether they're on a racquetball court or in a court of law, men prefer to come out on top. Whether they're on the putting green or comparing thc green in their wallets, the males of the human species are a pretty competitive lot.

This desire to win may be part of our fallen nature, the same type of pride that made Satan want to "ascend above the tops of the clouds" (Isaiah 14:14). But God can redeem even our competitive spirit, turning it toward victory over our own temptations and sin, by the power of the Lord Jesus Christ. Every true victory comes through Him.

But these victories come at a tremendously high price. They cost God the Father more than we could ever imagine.

When the apostle Paul told first-century Christians

in the city of Corinth, "you were bought at a price" (1 Corinthians 6:20), he was referring to Jesus as God Himself, becoming a man to provide the once-and-for-all sacrifice that covered our sins—every sin, of every person, of every place and time. Now, we can claim that victory by simply believing and receiving what God freely offers through Jesus Christ.

Let's respond to God in gratitude, acknowledging that these victories having nothing to do with us—what we've ever done or ever will do—and everything to do with Him. Let's enjoy the love that motivated God to give us the victory.

Gracious, generous, loving Father, thank You for promising me victory through Jesus Christ. Never let me forget the tremendous price You paid so that I could receive that promise.

BEAUTY

Worship the LORD in the beauty of holiness.

PSALM 29:2 NKJV

The biblical Rachel was acknowledged to be beautiful in form and appearance (Genesis 29:17). Abigail was known for her beauty (1 Samuel 25:3). And Queen Vashti was apparently something to see (Esther 1:11). Men do not have a difficult time noticing an attractive woman. Her beauty draws him in.

Today's verse describes a different kind of beauty, though it may include an element of the physical. Commentators point out that the language here may refer to the vestments worn by priests in the sanctuary when they stood in God's presence. But Psalm 29:2 also appears to mean that holiness has an inherent beauty. A popular Bible commentary of the nineteenth century makes this point: "In goodness and holiness of every kind there is a sweetness and grace which may well be called 'beauty,' seeing that it has a close analogy with the beautiful in external nature and in art."

Compare that to what the apostle Peter said to wives in 1 Peter 3:3–4: "Do not let your adornment be merely outward—arranging the hair, wearing gold, or putting on fine apparel—rather let it be the hidden person of the heart, with the incorruptible beauty of a gentle and quiet spirit, which is very precious in the sight of God."

Men can appreciate beauty in the physical world, whether in women or sunsets or even European sports cars. But there's a beauty in holiness that surpasses anything tangible. Why not begin a study of biblical holiness to guide your worship of God? You'll discover a beauty that is much more than skin deep.

Father, I know my worship often falls short.
Make it beautiful in holiness–in the qualities
that reflect Your goodness back upon You.

PRAYER

In the morning, LORD, you hear my voice; in the morning I lay my requests before you and wait expectantly.
PSALM 5:3 NIV

If you were to ask productivity experts "What is the most important thing to do each morning?" you would get a variety of answers. Their books on the morning routine discuss sleeping patterns, eating a good breakfast, avoiding technology, and using the early hours of each day for creative pursuits. Few of the books or experts mention prayer.

For Jesus, though, prayer was a staple. Mark 1:35 tells us, "Very early in the morning, while it was still dark, Jesus got up, left the house and went off to a solitary place, where he prayed." Though this is the only verse that specifically says Jesus prayed in the morning, we can imagine it was not a one-time occurrence. Why? Because Luke 5:16 says "Jesus often withdrew to lonely places and prayed."

For Jesus, prayer was not simply something sprinkled into the day—prayer was woven throughout its entirety. He communed with His Father and made His requests. Even now, He continues to pray on our behalf.

And as we pray, we can approach our heavenly Father as boldly as Jesus did. The apostle Paul wrote, "Who then is the one who condemns? No one. Christ Jesus who died—more than that, who was raised to life—is at the right hand of God and is also interceding for us" (Romans 8:34).

The practice of frequent daily prayer was (and still is) important to our Lord. It is something we must incorporate into our own lives.

Father, I thank You for hearing my prayers and for answering them according to Your great love for me.

LAUGHTER

Then our mouth was filled with laughter, and our tongue with shouts of joy; then they said among the nations, "The Lord *has done great things for them."*

PSALM 126:2 ESV

Why do people laugh? It may seem like a funny question, but it is something that philosophers have debated for millennia.

One early attempt to explain laughter was the superiority theory, which said people laughed in order to show their smugness. Think of high-society types laughing derisively at someone below their social status.

The prevailing theory today is the incongruity theory, which says the essence of humor is surprising others with something that doesn't fit. Think about stand-up comedians who set up a joke and then hit their listeners with an unexpected punchline. Our laughter is a recognition of surprise.

In reality, there are many reasons for people to laugh. The Bible actually shows some people who laughed for reasons of superiority. Remember Sarah chuckling at God's announcement that she would give birth in her old age? She thought she knew more than the God of the universe!

One instance where the incongruity theory applies is in today's verse, Psalm 126:2. God had just returned His chosen people from exile. He had given them goodness and blessing that they didn't deserve, and "our mouth was filled with laughter." This laughter is a kind of praise, and God's people wanted it to be heard around the world.

Have you ever been surprised by God's goodness in your life? Then laugh and give Him praise! God is always doing great things for you.

Lord, may my laughter be wholesome. I thank You for the great things You have done. May others see the blessings You give and laugh with me, because You are the God of good surprises.

EQUALITY

In this new life, it doesn't matter if you are a Jew or a Gentile, circumcised or uncircumcised, barbaric, uncivilized, slave, or free. Christ is all that matters, and he lives in all of us.

COLOSSIANS 3:11 NLT

Branch Rickey and Jackie Robinson broke Major League Baseball's color barrier in the late 1940s. Before that—and even for quite a while afterward—African-American stars played on traveling Negro League teams because the big leagues were so unwelcoming.

Some of the most talented players in history spent all or much of their careers in the Negro Leagues: Rube Foster, Satchel Paige, Josh Gibson, Oscar Charleston, John Henry "Pop" Lloyd, Buck Leonard, Turkey Stearnes, Cool Papa Bell. If you aren't familiar with their stories and accomplishments, look them up. They deserve to be remembered.

The historical prejudices of big league baseball—and much of American society—are sad reminders of human sinfulness. But you can be sure that the true Gospel of Jesus Christ has never tolerated such injustice. It doesn't matter if you are white or black, male or female, Jew or Gentile, rich or poor, slave or free—we're all equal in God's sight. We're all sinners in dire need of a Savior.

The church ought to be a model for equality, but that's not always the case. Sadly, many local churches are just as segregated as old-time baseball. What is your local fellowship doing to reach out to people of different backgrounds? What are you doing personally?

Father, I want my church to look like the kingdom will one day–filled with people from every tribe, tongue, and nation. Help me to reach out to others, especially those who aren't always treated fairly by the larger society.

FRUITFUL

That ye might walk worthy of the Lord unto all pleasing, being fruitful in every good work, and increasing in the knowledge of God.

COLOSSIANS 1:10 KJV

Jesus said every tree is known by its fruit (Luke 6:44). As believers, we all desire to be fruitful. And when we are connected to Jesus at the root, fruit happens naturally—it's the result of who we are. But it's important to remember that fruit does not appear the minute a seed falls into the soil. Even after a plant has grown for years, there's still a natural, beautiful rhythm of seasons as fruit is born and begins to mature.

The branch buds and flowers in one season. Its fruit springs to life in another. Finally, at the peak of a tree's strength, the fruit is harvested. Then the tree will lie dormant for a time, until the cycle starts over again.

Think about it: If you had to choose between *success* and *fruitfulness*, which would it be?

That beautiful tree in your backyard doesn't worry

about whether it's producing enough fruit. And we don't need to worry about that either. What season do you find yourself in today? Are you beginning to bud? Be patient and remember you still have a way to go. Are you finally bearing fruit? Thank God, who gave you your leaves and branches. Is it harvest time? Enjoy the rewards of a job well done. But know that ahead there will be a winter season of waiting, resting, and renewing your strength.

Thank You, Jesus, for seasons of new growth. Fruitful times are the result of my being grafted into the vine and knowing that all of my strength—every bit of it—comes from You.

POSSIBILITY

"With men this is impossible,
but with God all things are possible."
MATTHEW 19:26 NKJV

When first published in 1937, J. R. R. Tolkien's *The Hobbit* became a smashing success. Tolkien's audience (and his publisher) begged for a sequel.

Busy as a research fellow, however, Tolkien wrote the publisher on July 24, 1938, to say the requested sequel had only advanced a few chapters. He had no idea what to do with it next! Tolkien stated that *The Hobbit* was the complete story of Bilbo Baggins; its final sentence described Bilbo as happy until the end of his days, so a sequel was never intended. A follow-up was impossible to write.

At some point, all of us arrive at this place in life. We are faced with a difficult task, confronted by an obstacle that seems impossible to overcome. We can't see a way forward, and we know there is no way around. Still, in spite of the seeming impossibility, we are compelled to move onward. Someone—our wife, our children, our boss, perhaps even God—demands that we try.

God never promised that our plans would succeed. But when we follow the guidance of Ecclesiastes 9:10 (NASB)—"Whatever your hand finds to do, do it with all your might"—we can then leave the rest in His very capable hands. All things are possible for God.

Tolkien did eventually complete his sequel. When finished, it was one of the greatest fantasy adventures ever written. Can you imagine what book- and movie-lovers would have lost if the *Lord of the Rings* trilogy had been abandoned at the first "insuperable" obstacle?

Lord, no matter how impossible my situation may seem, I trust in You, and the fact that You can make the impossible possible.

DELIGHT

"I delight to do your will, O my God;
your law is within my heart."
PSALM 40:8 ESV

In a discussion of Jesus' sacrifice on the cross, the author of Hebrews said it was "impossible for the blood of bulls and goats to take away sins" (10:4). Those Old Testament sacrifices were limited in their effect, so Jesus came to make one perfect sacrifice that could cover every sin of all time.

Hebrews attributes the words of Psalm 40:8 to Christ, indicating that His awful death on the cross was also a delightful form of obedience. "Herein is the essence of obedience," the great English pastor Charles Spurgeon wrote, "namely, in the soul's cheerful devotion to God: and our Lord's obedience, which is our righteousness, is in no measure lacking in this eminent quality."

We can never fully express such perfect delight in our obedience, but we can exhibit some measure of it. For just as the law of the Lord was written in Christ's heart, it's in ours as well (Hebrews 10:16).

Pastor and author John Piper says Hebrews 10:16 is teaching that "when we are born again, God gives us a new heart and a new spirit, and the result is that the law of God written in Scripture is no longer offensive to us." Christians, then, are delighted to do God's commands.

We won't always feel such delight, because we're still being sanctified by God's Spirit. But has our overall attitude changed? The next time you find yourself struggling with obedience, use it as an opportunity to check your heart. Is there a sin you need to renounce?

Father, my sin often weighs me down. I confess that I don't always delight in doing Your will. But I want to, Lord. Make obedience my default setting.

FOLLOWING

He who follows righteousness and mercy
finds life, righteousness, and honor.
PROVERBS 21:21 NKJV

If you want to know how to live, you'll get plenty of guidance from the Proverbs. Every chapter includes wisdom for daily life, but Proverbs 21 is particularly helpful. It details what the Lord looks for when He surveys our lives.

The most critical verse is perhaps the twenty-first, which says, "He who follows righteousness and mercy finds life, righteousness, and honor." It's safe to say that "life, righteousness, and honor" are all things that we want to attain, right? So, then, how do we "follow righteousness and mercy"?

For an answer, let's turn to Jesus' words in Matthew 6:33. There, as part of His "sermon on the mount," the Lord told us to "*seek first* the kingdom of God" (emphasis added). In everything we do—whether our jobs or marriages or hobbies or ministries or whatever—our attention and intent should be set on "things above" (Colossians 3:2). Then, when we die, we will also appear with Jesus Christ in glory (Colossians 3:4).

We can only focus on things above after we've truly repented, when we submit to the will of the Father, turning everything over to Him and His plan.

It's definitely going to be a challenge. We will slip and fall. But the Lord will guide and help us as long as our desire is to completely follow Him. When we do that, He will bless us with life, righteousness, and honor.

Lord, my desire is to follow You in righteousness and mercy. Keep my eyes fixed on You, I pray. May I ultimately find life, righteousness, and honor.

GUIDANCE

"When the Spirit of truth comes, he will guide you into all the truth, for he will not speak on his own authority, but whatever he hears he will speak, and he will declare to you the things that are to come."

JOHN 16:13 ESV

Grab a Bible concordance and look up the word *internet*. Actually, save yourself the time—it isn't in there. Here are a few other things that the Bible doesn't mention by name: pickup trucks, muzzleloaders, and hockey. Why would the Bible be silent on important topics like these?

The truth is that even though God didn't mention this stuff in the Bible by name, He still cares about each and gives us guidance on them.

The internet is a tool for "researching" anything we can imagine. But God still warns us to protect our eyes. In the Sermon on the Mount, Jesus said, "You have heard that it was said, 'You shall not commit adultery.' But I say to you that everyone who looks at a woman with lustful intent has already committed adultery with her in his heart" (Matthew 5:27–28).

Not only did He give us principles to live by, God gave us the Holy Spirit as a personal guide. It doesn't matter that "pickup trucks" aren't mentioned in the Bible. We have the Holy Spirit to remind us to treat other drivers with respect.

What about muzzleloaders and hockey? Pray about it. Ask the Spirit to guide you. He will because God said He will.

Lord, I thank You for the Spirit of truth. Give me ears to hear Him speak. Thank You for the Bible. Give me a desire to live by its truth.

GROWTH

The righteous shall flourish like the palm tree: he shall grow like a cedar in Lebanon.

PSALM 92:12 KJV

"Don't cry because it's over—smile because it happened." So said Dr. Seuss.

No, Dr. Seuss was not a real doctor. But the medicine that Theodore Geisel prescribed is still making the world a happier place. He wrote his final book, *Oh the Places You'll Go*, at age eighty-six. He was still green. Still growing. Still looking ahead.

That's what it means to grow. The ultimate purpose of growth is not a goal or destination. Growth is simply a journey. All living things are growing things.

Do you ever think about your own faith journey? It's easy to get so focused on our destination that we miss the beauty all around us as we travel. Let's remember that the destination is just a part of our Christian journey. The beauty we often miss—the entire point of being alive in the first place—*is Jesus Himself.*

Have you stopped growing? Maybe it's time to check your soil. Here is how Jesus Himself put it: "Behold, a sower went forth to sow; and when he sowed, some seeds fell by the way side, and the fowls came and devoured them up: some fell upon stony places, where they had not much earth: and forthwith they sprung up, because they had no deepness of earth: and when the sun was up, they were scorched; and because they had no root, they withered away. And some fell among thorns; and the thorns sprung up, and choked them: but other fell into good ground, and brought forth fruit, some an hundredfold, some sixtyfold, some thirtyfold" (Matthew 13:3–8).

Jesus, may I keep my focus on You today—and flourish like a palm tree.

COMFORT

For whatsoever things were written aforetime were written for our learning, that we through patience and comfort of the scriptures might have hope.

ROMANS 15:4 KJV

A few years back, a Wisconsin newspaper included the obituary of a thirty-nine-year-old man who passed away after battling a neurological disease.

As is usual, the death notice provided a few details about the man's life, including where he was born and the fact that he was the youngest of six children. But then there was a mention of what helped him through his illness: "Brad was a loving son, brother, and uncle who enjoyed following sports and finding joy in life, including attending a dance even in declining health," the obituary said. "He loved reading the Bible and found great comfort in Jesus as he grappled with his illness."

The Bible is important in so many ways. Romans 15:4 says God's Word was recorded for our learning, "that we through patience and comfort of the scriptures we might have hope."

Where do you turn for comfort and hope? Self-help books, the accumulation of wealth, or even physical fitness? Or do you find peace and strength in God's Word? The apostle Paul would not discourage learning new things, providing for your family, and working to stay healthy. But he knew our eternal comfort and hope can come only from Jesus—and until He returns to earth, we encounter Him in the scriptures.

Immersing yourself in the Bible prepares you for anything—even a diagnosis like Brad's. If you aren't in the habit of daily Bible reading, start now.

Father, I know that my hope and comfort are to be found in the scriptures, but I sometimes allow the cares of this world to overwhelm me. Give me a hunger for Your Word.

QUIET

The words of the wise heard in quiet are better than the shouting of a ruler among fools.
ECCLESIASTES 9:17 ESV

Is it ever completely and totally quiet where you are? Not likely. Most of us are bombarded with noise throughout our daily existence. At home, it's the television or YouTube. In the car, it's music or talk radio. At the office, it's chatty coworkers or the next big meeting. Where is the quiet?

It's been said regarding time that we can never *find* time for some important task—we have to *make* it. The same is true of quiet. In this world, if you want peaceful times and places, you'll need to intentionally pursue them.

The Gospels show us this pattern in the life of Jesus Christ. In spite of the demands of His work—especially the hundreds and thousands of people He encountered—Jesus also made time to be alone and quiet. His quiet times varied from a few minutes to as many as forty days (Matthew 4:1–2). Jesus did this to tune out the noise of everyday life and instead to listen for the voice of the heavenly Father.

And the Lord invited His twelve disciples—as He invites us today—to do the same: "Come away by yourselves to a desolate place and rest a while" (Mark 6:31).

Perhaps we need to turn off the rulers and fools shouting from cable television and the car radio and our social media feeds. Let's devote some serious, *quiet* time to listening to the words of the One who is wise.

Heavenly Father, help me to create that quiet space where I can hear Your voice. I need to hear from You, Lord.

MONEY

"No one can serve two masters. Either you will hate the one and love the other, or you will be devoted to the one and despise the other. You cannot serve both God and money."

LUKE 16:13 NIV

The band Casting Crowns released a self-titled album in October 2003. At thc number five spot was "American Dream," a song that depicts a man whose unhealthy obsession with his job and earnings took priority over his family and his relationship with Jesus. The song begins: "All work no play may have made Jack a dull boy. But, all work no God has left Jack with a lost soul." Immediately, we can see the danger that Jack's priority creates.

In Luke 16, Jesus told a story that some call "the Parable of the Unjust Steward." The Lord pulled no punches when He said, "You *cannot* serve both God and money." Jesus has presented all of us with a choice: we are forced to decide what is of most importance to us. What (or *whom*) will we serve?

Casting Crowns described Jack's "American dream" as more like a nightmare, and if we're honest, we can probably see the truth of that in our own lives. Living for the pursuit of money and things leads only to a never-ending expectation of more—plus stress, burnout, and defeat. Why? Because, as Jesus went on to say, "What people value highly is detestable in God's sight" (Luke 16:14).

So, who will you serve?

Dear Jesus, I confess that it is very easy to put my focus on making more money. May my attention and desire be only on You, knowing that You will provide for all my needs. Help me to trust and obey as I follow You. Amen.

PATIENCE

Sensible people control their temper;
they earn respect by overlooking wrongs.
PROVERBS 19:11 NLT

Have you ever heard of Stanislav Yevgrafovich Petrov? On September 26, 1983, he likely prevented a nuclear war between the United States and the Soviet Union.

To say that relations between the two countries had been tense would be an understatement. During the Cold War, bomb shelters were built, schools conducted drills to prepare for an attack, and the US and USSR studied each other like chess masters in a high-stakes game.

Colonel Petrov was in charge of the Soviets' nuclear early warning system when it reported a small number of missiles had launched from the United States. Policies and procedures, pressure from subordinates, and the advanced weapons system told Petrov to alert the highest levels of the Soviet military and government, which would likely respond with their own missiles. Petrov's training, however, had indicated that any attack would be on a massive scale to prevent a counterstrike. He concluded the warning system had malfunctioned—which happily proved to be true.

How different the world would be today if Colonel Petrov had simply reacted toward his enemy rather than patiently thinking the situation through. It's easy to become angry and retaliatory toward others, but that's not God's way. "Better to be patient than powerful," the scriptures say. "Better to have self-control than to conquer a city" (Proverbs 16:32 NLT).

Next time you feel the pressure rising, remember Stanislav Petrov. Patience can stave off a nuclear disaster in your own life and relationships.

Lord, I know I will face challenging situations today. May You provide the patience and wisdom I need to respond in a way that brings honor to You.

CONVERSATION

Let your conversation be gracious and attractive so that you will have the right response for everyone.

COLOSSIANS 4:6 NLT

In this verse, the apostle Paul advises Christians on their conversations with unbelievers. (You can see verse 5 for more context.) But what exactly do "gracious and attractive" conversations look like? The English Standard Version of the Bible renders the verse this way: "Let your speech always be gracious, seasoned with salt." Does that help?

When used with food, salt is both a preservative and a flavor enhancer. You might remember what Jesus said about salt in Matthew 5:13 (NLT): "You are the salt of the earth. But what good is salt if it has lost its flavor? Can you make it salty again? It will be thrown out and trampled underfoot as worthless."

If we as Christians engage the world in gracious, attractive, "salty" conversations, unbelievers will hear the truth. Our words should "taste" different than those they are accustomed to. Our words should have a lasting, preservative effect. Ideally, our conversation should give the world pause, perhaps to the point where people reconsider their sprint toward the wide gate that leads to destruction (Matthew 7:13).

If your words are going to have this sort of impact, you'll have to be intentional. And you'll have to be willing to be considered odd. But never forget that you have the words of eternal life. Redemption is on your lips. Speak the truth graciously to anyone who will listen, and wait for God to do the rest.

Father, I can be timid in matters of faith while conversing with unbelievers. Remind me that Your Spirit is ready and waiting to give me words when I don't know what to say.

KINDNESS

For His merciful kindness is great toward us, and the truth of the LORD endures forever. Praise the LORD!

PSALM 117:2 NKJV

With four decades on television and a name that is still revered around the world, Fred Rogers of *Mister Rogers' Neighborhood* knew what it was to be successful. He once said, "There are three ways to ultimate success: The first way is to be kind. The second way is to be kind. The third way is to be kind."

Kindness may be one of the least discussed virtues. In a world where power is conflated with strength, it is often confused for weakness. The truth is that kindness *requires* strength. Kindness is hard to give, especially to those people who don't seem to deserve it. Only the strong are equipped to be kind.

The writer of Psalm 117 knew about strength and kindness. This short psalm is a call for the whole world to rejoice in the kindness of the strongest being in the universe—God. What kindness should we praise Him for? Well, for every good thing He does. . .but we can start with His mercy to all people, to every rebellious human being who deserves wrath instead of love.

Are you ready to be as kind to the undeserving as God has been to you? Are you ready to step up and test your strength? Fred Rogers, who was also a Presbyterian minister, knew that kindness was the only way to succeed in spreading God's love.

How can you be kind today?

Lord, help me to be kind. Give me an opportunity today to show others the mercy that You have shown to me. Please make me strong enough to do this every day.

REFRESHED

Repent ye therefore, and be converted, that your sins may be blotted out, when the times of refreshing shall come from the presence of the Lord.

ACTS 3:19 KJV

In the film *The Shawshank Redemption*, banker Andy Dufresne is convicted of murdering his wife and her lover. Though he maintains his innocence, he is sentenced to life in the dreary Shawshank State Penitentiary.

After a horrendous introduction to prison, Andy slowly ingratiates himself with the guards and warden, using his financial background to help them—both legally and otherwise. Over the next two decades at Shawshank, he sets up the crooked warden and devises a plan to access his ill-gotten money. Then Andy makes a harrowing escape through the sewer and ultimately settles on a beach in Mexico.

By the movie's end, when his recently-released prison buddy Red joins him in Mexico, Andy has clearly changed. He no longer wears dirty prison overalls but shorts and an unbuttoned shirt. Best of all, he no longer sports his deep, perpetual frown but smiles warmly as Red approaches. It's a cinematic hint of the kind of change God makes in our lives.

The Lord longs to refresh His people. By His death on the cross, Jesus took the punishment for our sins—as well as the burden of the spiritual and physical pain that sin creates. Jesus' work is a fulfillment of the prophet Jeremiah's words, "I will refresh the weary and satisfy the faint" (Jeremiah 31:25 NIV).

This is a promise all Christians can claim. When we repent—when we turn away from our sins and to God—times of refreshing will flow from the Lord.

Lord, I thank You for the blood of Jesus that cleanses my sins. I can be refreshed each day.

VALUE

Fear ye not therefore, ye are of more value than many sparrows.

MATTHEW 10:31 KJV

Someone has pointed out that when God made the universe and all the incredible things in it, He demonstrated His power and creativity. But when He created human beings, He demonstrated His love.

Of all creation, only one thing was "in the image of God": humankind. The Bible says that God gave Adam special treatment. Rather than speaking him into existence like everything else, God formed Adam from the dust. Then He "breathed into his nostrils the breath of life, and the man became a living being" (Genesis 2:7 NIV).

When we consider how uniquely God created human beings, we catch a glimpse of our value in His eyes. Then Jesus made that perfectly clear, telling His followers, "Are not two sparrows sold for a penny? Yet not one of them will fall to the ground outside your Father's care. And even the very hairs of your head are all numbered. So don't be afraid; you are worth more than many sparrows" (Matthew 10:29–31 NIV).

In fact, we human beings are so valuable to God that He gave His one and only Son, Jesus, to die on a cross for our sins. And when we simply believe in Jesus' sacrifice, God can restore us to the purpose for which we were made in the first place—perfect, loving fellowship with Him.

God loves and values us, so He gave. . .and then gave some more. That's just what God's love does.

Loving Father, I thank You for valuing me so much more than I can even understand. I know my value to You has nothing to do with any good within me. It's just because You are the very personification of love.

JOKING

Neither filthiness, nor foolish talking,
nor coarse jesting, which are not
fitting, but rather giving of thanks.
EPHESIANS 5:4 NKJV

Have you ever heard a joke that made you cringe? What about a joke that caused emotional pain to someone? Have you ever heard—or maybe even told—a story that caused you to reconsider your involvement in it? The apostle Paul tells us not to be involved in such things at all. Rather, we should use our speech to give thanks!

Ed was a hardworking, quiet, respectful young man. His wife and two sons were his world, though he was also involved in several charities and helped with the youth ministry at his church. The most challenging thing for Ed was his work environment. He repaired heavy machinery at a diesel mechanic shop, where the other guys were loud, boisterous, and crude.

One day, Ed was tasked with training Jason, a new guy. As the other men in the shop joked, telling their typically inappropriate stories and making fun of different people, Jason took notice of Ed. He was refusing to involve himself and instead focused on doing his work well and keeping his attitude positive. When Jason asked why he acted so differently, Ed had an opportunity to share Jesus with him.

First John 2:6 says, "He who says he abides in [Jesus] ought himself also to walk just as He walked." Do you think Jesus ever told off-color jokes or made fun of others? No—but He often gave thanks.

Let's do the same. It may be a challenge, but it's well worth the end result!

Father, I commit myself to giving thanks. If an inappropriate comment or joke crosses my mind, I ask you to slay it. In Jesus' name, amen.

WHOLEHEARTED

And ye shall seek me, and find me, when ye shall search for me with all your heart.
JEREMIAH 29:13 KJV

There is no greater stage for sports than the football (in the United States, *soccer*) tournament known as the World Cup. In the 2018 edition, a semifinal match pitted the traditional power England against an emerging team from Croatia. England was favored to win, but the upstart Croatians prevailed 2–1 in overtime.

You would think sportswriters and commentators would focus on the winning team, but the obvious star of the match was England's captain, Harry Kane. For 120 minutes, Kane did everything within his considerable abilities to lift his national team to victory. Following the loss, manager Gareth Southgate would say of Kane, "I think he has given everything for the team"—not just against Croatia but throughout his long career. Harry Kane was wholehearted.

And so was the prophet Jeremiah, the human author of

today's verse. Despite confrontations with false prophets, plots against his life, beatings, and imprisonment (he was held in a muddy cistern), Jeremiah maintained his dedication to the work God had given him. Today, he is celebrated in Christianity, Judaism, and even Islam—and he is the ideal man to encourage us with the command to search for the Lord "with all your heart."

Wholeheartedness comes at a price—it wasn't easy for either Jeremiah or Harry Kane. But the alternative is halfheartedness, which just sounds pathetic. Seek God wholeheartedly, and He promises you'll find Him. And whatever hardships you experience will be worth it.

Dear Lord, place within me the desire to seek after You wholeheartedly. May I be dedicated to searching for You in every part of my life so I can serve in a way that pleases You.

FAITH

Now faith is confidence in what we hope for and assurance about what we do not see.
HEBREWS 11:1 NIV

The Voice of the Martyrs website reports that Christians are currently being persecuted in more than forty nations around the world. "Those who boldly follow Christ—in spite of government edict or radical opposition—can face harassment, arrest, torture and even death," the organization says. "Yet Christians continue to meet for worship and to witness for Christ, and the church in restricted nations is growing."

Why would these believers keep meeting for worship and continue to witness for Christ? Why are they willing to face harassment, arrest, torture, or death? Because their faith offers them confidence in what they hope for and assurance about what they do not see. God has bigger and better things for them (and us) than just this world.

Notice that faith and hope go hand in hand. The Christian's faith infuses him with confidence, hope, and assurance, both in the here and now and for eternity.

Few of us in the West face persecution, besides a little harassment or mockery. Do you find yourself backpedaling when the world wants to know what you believe? Is your faith infusing you with confidence, hope, and assurance? If it crumbles under light pressure, it will not hold up when greater persecution comes.

So shore up your faith now. Feast on God's Word. Surround yourself with strong, believing brothers. Devote yourself to periods of prayer and reflection. In so doing, you can have confidence—that your faith will be able to withstand anything.

Father, I marvel when I hear about the hardships that other Christians around the world endure for Your name's sake. Prepare me to be like them, O Lord.

REJOICING

Exult in his holy name; rejoice,
you who worship the LORD.
1 CHRONICLES 16:10 NLT

In 1914, Sir Ernest Shackleton led a crew to Antarctica with the aim of crossing the continent by way of the South Pole. In early 1915, though, their ship became trapped in the unforgiving Antarctic ice. *Endurance* was ultimately crushed and sank beneath the frigid waters. Shackleton and his men were stranded on floating ice.

They took three small boats salvaged from the ship and made their way to nearby Elephant Island. From there, Shackleton and five men sailed in one of the boats for South Georgia Island, hoping to find help at a whaling station. They faced a journey of eight hundred miles. Happily, after sixteen days, the group reached their destination.

In August 1916, well over a year later, Shackleton returned to Elephant Island wondering what he would find—his crew or their remains. Amazingly, he counted every one of his men alive and waiting for him.

We can only imagine the elation of Ernest Shackleton and his crew in that moment. Like so many of the memorable events of history, it goes far beyond our everyday experience. But rejoicing should be a part of our lives in big moments and small. As the Old Testament prophet Joel put it, "Be glad, people of Zion, rejoice in the LORD your God, for he has given you the autumn rains because he is faithful. He sends you abundant showers, both autumn and spring rains, as before" (Joel 2:23 NIV).

Every day brings some reason for rejoicing. . .our job is simply to find it. What can you thank and praise God for this day?

Lord, I celebrate and praise You for all the ways You have provided for me.

LOVE

But the Holy Spirit produces this kind of fruit in our lives: love, joy, peace, patience, kindness, goodness, faithfulness, gentleness, and self-control.
GALATIANS 5:22–23 NLT

In a letter to one of his compatriots, founding father George Washington wrote, "It is unfortunate when men cannot, or will not, see danger at a distance; or seeing it, are restrained in the means which are necessary to avert, or keep it afar off. . . . Offensive operations, often times, is the *surest*, if not the *only* (in some cases) means of defence."

The adage is familiar to modern sports fans: the best defense is a good offense. Keep the ball on the other team's side of the field. Take the fight to them.

When the apostle Paul wrote his letter to the Galatians, he advised the believers on the offensive strategy of the Holy Spirit. Paul warned his readers that the desires of the flesh would destroy them but noted that the fruit of the Holy Spirit gives life.

This may sound like a passive system, but each of the fruits are part of the offense. They are both the result and the means of winning the fight against our worldly desires. Listed as first and greatest in the Christian's arsenal is love.

Loving another person takes our focus off ourselves. It actively chooses the best for someone else. When you love someone, you show them respect, patience, and kindness. And when things get tough, you stand by them. Love is the attribute that most clearly reflects the character of God.

Are you armed and ready to take the offense against sin? Fire away—with love.

Lord, help me to love like You love. May the Holy Spirit produce Your fruits in my life, starting with love.

UNFAILING

The Lord*'s lovingkindnesses indeed never cease, for His compassions never fail.*

LAMENTATIONS 3:22 NASB

Could you depend on anyone 100 percent of the time? Could anyone depend on you like that?

We know that the people in our lives—even those who love us dearly—will fail us at times, just as we will fail them. We're all fallen humans, and we're more than capable of responding to one another in unloving, impatient, and ungracious ways. That's why the Bible tells us, "As God's chosen people, holy and dearly loved, clothe yourselves with compassion, kindness, humility, gentleness and patience. Bear with each other and forgive one another if any of you has a grievance against someone. Forgive as the Lord forgave you" (Colossians 3:12–13 NIV).

But there *is* one person we can depend on completely, one person who will never let us down, one person who loves with an unfailing love: our heavenly Father. If you were to search the New International Version of the Bible, you'd find that the phrase "unfailing love" applied to God dozens of times, including more than thirty times in the Psalms alone.

Isn't it comforting to know that God loves us unfailingly?

Yes, there are times when God feels anger, sorrow, or frustration toward His own people. But His love and kindness will never fail, even when we stray from His best for us.

You can always count on God's love and faithfulness. He'll never disappoint you or let you down. And He'll always love you. . .without fail!

Lord God, I thank You for showing Yourself absolutely dependable in so many ways, including Your love for me. Your love never fails, even in those times when I fail You.

MERCY

Surely goodness and mercy shall follow me all the days of my life: and I will dwell in the house of the LORD *for ever.*

PSALM 23:6 KJV

The Twenty-Third Psalm is pretty famous. It is recited at funerals. It is quoted in movies. It can be found in songs from Duke Ellington, Pink Floyd, U2, Tupac Shakur, Kanye West, and many other artists. Though it is familiar, it deserves a second look.

The psalm uses two sets of imagery from the life of its author, King David. The first picture harkens back to young David's days as a shepherd. It refers to God as a good shepherd who cares for His sheep, protecting them from harm and leading them to comfort. This picture is one of love and care.

The second picture is from much later in David's life. It shows a victory feast in the aftermath of a battle. It is a picture of mercy.

Imagine that you are a soldier who has been captured

by the enemy. You expect to be interrogated, mistreated, perhaps even killed. Instead, you are taken to the king's table, placed in a seat of honor, and treated as a royal son.

This is exactly the mercy that God has shown to us.

We were born in enemy territory, and we lived as enemies of righteousness. But then we were captured by God's love. Now our cups run over with blessing, because Jesus volunteered to take the punishment we deserved.

Give thanks today for God's mercy!

Father God, I thank You for loving me when I don't deserve it. Thank You for capturing me from the enemy and allowing me to sit at Your table. Help me to show Your mercy to others in my life.

STRENGTH

That is why, for Christ's sake, I delight in weaknesses, in insults, in hardships, in persecutions, in difficulties. For when I am weak, then I am strong.

2 CORINTHIANS 12:10 NIV

Brooklyn's Angelo Siciliano didn't delight in weakness or insults. Visiting the beach in the early twentieth century, the young Italian immigrant had a bully kick sand in his face. The self-described "ninety-seven-pound weakling" took action: he began seeking the most effective body-building plan.

Before long, he discovered "Dynamic Tension," a technique pitting the body's muscles against each other to generate strength and bulk. Siciliano grew both physically and in fame, changing his name to Charles Atlas and selling his method to other guys. His advertisements, commonly appearing in comic books, featured headlines such as "The Insult That Made a Man Out of Mac."

Most of us want to be strong physically, emotionally,

and spiritually. But life is often much harder than we expect—accidents and diseases, relationship issues, and moral temptations prove that we're not quite as tough as we'd hoped. But that's okay, according to scripture. The apostle Paul, who faced his share of trials, ultimately realized that weakness was simply an opportunity for God's strength to flow through him.

In 2 Corinthians 12, Paul wrote of a mysterious "thorn in the flesh" that he asked God to remove. But the Lord answered *no* three times, saying, "My grace is sufficient for you, for my power is made perfect in weakness." Paul's response? "Therefore I will boast all the more gladly about my weaknesses, so that Christ's power may rest on me" (verse 9).

Don't try to be a spiritual Charles Atlas. God has all the strength you need.

Father, may I never rely on my own strength. Help me to rest in Your unlimited power.

SEASONS

To everything there is a season, a time for every purpose under heaven.
ECCLESIASTES 3:1 NKJV

Whether they realize it or not, millions of people have memorized scripture thanks to Pete Seeger. His song "Turn, Turn, Turn," made famous in 1965 by a band called the Byrds, came straight out of Ecclesiastes 3:1–8.

Seeger experienced many dramatic seasons in his life. Born in 1919, drafted during World War II, a participant in many civil rights movements of the 1960s, and elected into the Rock and Roll Hall of Fame in 1996, he passed away in 2014 at the age of ninety-four.

Some would say his views on politics and religion were extreme, but Seeger felt that his primary responsibility in life was to make the world a better place. "Turn, Turn, Turn" was a testimony to that pursuit—and a reminder to all of us how regularly life changes.

New seasons happen when we get married, start a career, or have children. Other seasons are harder, if we lose a loved one, a job, or our health. We find ourselves reacting differently to each one, often experiencing a "fight-or-flight" response: we may readily face the new season and take its challenges head on, or we feel apprehensive of the change and want to run in the other direction.

The apostle Paul tells us exactly how to react to new seasons of life, whether good or bad: "Rejoice always, pray continually, give thanks in all circumstances; for this is God's will for you in Christ Jesus" (1 Thessalonians 5:16–18 NIV). That's how you "turn, turn, turn" any season of life into a closer connection with God.

Lord, no matter what the seasons bring,
may You provide strength for endurance
and wisdom for the choices I make.

OPTIMISM

Why are you cast down, O my soul, and why are you in turmoil within me? Hope in God; for I shall again praise him, my salvation and my God.

PSALM 42:11 ESV

Besides his improvements to calculus, the binary system, and mechanical calculators, Gottfried Wilhelm Leibniz (1646–1716) made a major contribution to philosophy. In fact, he might be considered the father of optimism. In his book *The Theodicy*, Leibniz contended that this world is the best of all possible worlds.

In his lifetime, Leibniz's ideas were lampooned by the French writer Voltaire as being simplistic and dangerously fatalistic. If this is the best of all possible worlds, Voltaire might ask, then should man simply accept his faults as preordained or should he work to make things better?

Christians are often caught in the middle of this quandary. We know that God is perfect, but we live in an obviously imperfect world. We experience suffering and cry out for God's deliverance, but our suffering may not end. How can we be optimistic in such a pessimistic place?

The answer is simply this: our hope is not in a mystical belief that "things will work out well in the end." Our hope is in a God who loves us, who suffered as one of us, and who is actively working to redeem us. "Optimism" does not mean, as Voltaire feared, that we can kick back and watch the world go by. Our hope in God should lead us to good works, to redeeming those things that He has put into our power.

Why are you cast down, O my soul? Hope (optimistically) in God!

Lord, I thank You for working all things for Your good. Help me to work alongside You. Be my hope today and every day.

PEACE

Since we have been made right in God's sight by faith, we have peace with God because of what Jesus Christ our Lord has done for us.
ROMANS 5:1 NLT

In the final moments of the Marvel film *Captain America: The First Avenger*, the title hero is faced with a dilemma. What else would you expect from a superhero film?

Captain America has defeated the Red Skull but is now alone aboard a bomb-laden plane hurtling toward New York City. Thus, the comic book hero acts in a fittingly Captain America way: over the radio, he says good-bye to the woman he loves, then wrestles the plane's controls to send himself and the bomb to the bottom of the ocean. In the process, he loses his life while saving the lives of millions of New Yorkers. Even in fictional settings, peace comes at a cost. Peace for some is gained through the sacrifice of another.

This is the example we have from Jesus Christ.

Human beings can do nothing to *earn* peace with

God. But there is a Hero who is willing to *give* us the peace we long for. As the apostle Paul told his protégé, the young pastor Timothy, "There is one God and one Mediator who can reconcile God and humanity—the man Christ Jesus" (1 Timothy 2:5 NLT).

Though we can serve in church, read our Bibles and pray, or even do "random acts of kindness," we can never earn peace with God. The good news of the Gospel is this: while we were in rebellion against God, He brought peace through the sacrifice of His Son, Jesus.

Father, thank You for sending Your Son as a sacrifice for me. I know it is only through Him—not by my own actions—that I have peace with You.

REWARD

O love the L*ORD, all ye his saints: for the* L*ORD preserveth the faithful, and plentifully rewardeth the proud doer.*

PSALM 31:23 KJV

For a boxer, the perfect entrance song can help to focus his mind as he prepares for a match. The entrance can be slow and stoic or bombastic and celebratory. The latter was the case in January 2010 when Usman "Uzzy" Ahmed paraded down the aisle toward the ring.

Usman danced, gyrated, and pointed to his chest in what one sportswriter called "an incredibly annoying ring entrance." Usman continued his pompous antics as he stepped through the ropes to face Ashley Sexton. His confident posture suggested that he was certain of the outcome of the fight.

In the first round, however, Sexton landed a strong punch to Usman's chin, knocking him unconscious. Not surprisingly, a YouTube clip of Usman's dance and knock-out has been watched hundreds of thousands of times.

When a cocksure athlete is humbled, many of us can't help but celebrate the justice that has been served. After all, the Bible does not encourage arrogance of any kind. We should be careful, though, as scripture also says, "Beloved, never avenge yourselves, but leave it to the wrath of God, for it is written, 'Vengeance is mine, I will repay, says the Lord' " (Romans 12:19 ESV).

As the ultimate standard of goodness, only God has the authority to administer justice. If you ever feel inclined to hand out "rewards" of your own, don't. Remember that the Lord has promised to take care of His faithful people and "plentifully" pay back the proud as He sees fit.

Father, please prune my heart of arrogance and empower me to be true to You. I want to work toward Your heavenly reward.

SAVED

If you declare with your mouth, "Jesus is Lord," and believe in your heart that God raised him from the dead, you will be saved.
ROMANS 10:9 NIV

We've all seen well-meaning street preachers, shouting into megaphones and holding up signs that say something like "Repent or perish!" and "Jesus saves from hell!" When most Christians think of the word *saved*, they probably focus on what we're saved from—and what we want others to be saved from—namely, eternal punishment for our sin. And it's true that being "saved" means escaping God's judgment for our rebellion against Him. After all, the Bible repeatedly warns people about a terrible place called hell, calling them to turn to Jesus for salvation.

But scripture also teaches that being saved means the assurance of a blessed life here on earth followed by an eternity in what Jesus once called "paradise" (Luke 23:43). In other words, God doesn't just save us *from* something, He saves us *for* something.

The apostle Paul wrote, "We are God's handiwork, created in Christ Jesus to do good works, which God prepared in advance for us to do" (Ephesians 2:10). Think about that: God saved each one of us for some specific good work—work that He prepared for us long before we were ever born. And we perform those good works by serving others, acting as God's ambassadors to the world (2 Corinthians 5:20).

That's the blessed life of the saved on earth—a privilege far beyond anything our finite human minds could imagine. And then there's still eternity in heaven with God!

Lord Jesus, I thank You for saving me from eternal punishment for my sins. I thank You even more for saving me for blessed work on this earth and an eternity in paradise with You.

PROMISES

Through these he has given us his very great and precious promises, so that through them you may participate in the divine nature, having escaped the corruption in the world caused by evil desires.

2 PETER 1:4 NIV

In the spring of 1994, the NHL's New York Rangers faced the New Jersey Devils in the Eastern Conference final of the Stanley Cup playoffs. During the regular season, the teams had met six times, and the Rangers had bested New Jersey in every game. Unfortunately for New York, the Devils had found their stride at playoff time. They split the first four games with the Rangers, then won Game 5 to claim a 3–2 series lead.

With Game 6 headed back to New Jersey, Rangers captain Mark Messier thought it was time to take a stand. "We will win tonight," he told reporters.

As the first period ended, New York was down 2–0, and it appeared their captain was wrong. But in the third, Messier scored three goals to lead his team to victory.

The Rangers went on to win Game 7 and then its next series, to bring the Stanley Cup to New York City.

It's a great story, isn't it? But there are many other instances of sports promises that end differently. Thankfully, there's never a question about God's promises. What was true in Joshua's day is always true: "Not one of all the LORD's good promises to Israel failed; every one was fulfilled" (Joshua 21:45).

The One in whom we place our hope will never let us down. The promises we have in His Word cannot fail.

Father, I know that Your promises never fail. Thank You for Your faithfulness to me.

CONFESSION

Therefore confess your sins to each other and pray for each other so that you may be healed. The prayer of a righteous person is powerful and effective.

JAMES 5:16 NIV

Confessing sin to another Christian can be one of the most intimidating things you will ever do. It means being vulnerable, open, and honest about what is going on in your heart, mind, and body. It means you will not settle for staying mired in sin. It means being willing to live out your faith in Christian community, recognizing that true spiritual growth is most likely to occur in such fertile soil.

While the Bible writer James put it succinctly—"confess your sins to each other"—the sixteenth-century reformer Martin Luther expanded on the idea: "If anyone is wrestling with his sins and wants to be rid of them and desires a sure word on the matter, let him go and confess to another in secret, and accept what he says to him as if God himself had spoken it through the mouth of this person."

That's not to say you should confess your sin to any and every Christian you come across. But within the context of a safe Christian community, find a man with whom you can be honest—someone who will not judge you but help you stay on the narrow path. And then be willing to do the same for him. It will probably be uncomfortable at first. But as you encourage and pray for each other, James says you'll both experience healing.

Father, send me a Christian man I can trust, someone who will walk alongside me as I confess my sin. Make me the type of man who will offer the same safe harbor to him.

ENJOYMENT

Trust in. . .the living God, who giveth us richly all things to enjoy.

1 TIMOTHY 6:17 KJV

Every good and perfect gift comes from above (James 1:17), and there are a lot of them—family, friendships, hobbies, careers, even our dogs and cats. Of course, that's not to imply that the Christian life is always smooth sailing; scripture never shies away from the fact that faithful saints may indeed face martyrdom at some point. But, generally speaking, God calls His people to trust Him because He gives us all things to enjoy.

An old-time Bible commentator connected the dots between trusting in God and enjoyment. "The meaning of this seems to be," said Albert Barnes (1798–1870), "that God permits us to enjoy everything. Everything in the works of creation and redemption he has given to man for his happiness, and he should therefore trust in him."

Lest that feels too earthy at first glance, consider what Jesus Himself said in Matthew 7:9–11: "What man is there of you, whom if his son ask bread, will he give him a stone? Or if he ask a fish, will he give him a serpent? If ye then, being evil, know how to give good gifts unto your children, how much more shall your Father which is in heaven give good things to them that ask him?"

Indeed, God, whom you can trust, has given you "all things to enjoy"—richly. How does that jibe with your perception of God? How might 1 Timothy 6:17 affect your outlook today?

Father, I thank You for earnestly desiring to give Your children good things, things that we can enjoy. When I consider that, how can I do anything other than trust You?

SONGS

Sing to the L*ORD* *a new song;*
sing to the L*ORD*, *all the earth.*
PSALM 96:1 NIV

A little over a century ago, archaeologists made an amazing find at a dig near Oxyrhynchus, Egypt: the oldest known music notation and lyrics of a Christian hymn, dating to the late third century. It's amazing that a song of praise more than seventeen hundred years old has somehow made its way into modern culture. But the Oxyrhynchus hymn is far from the oldest praise song ever sung.

In the first century, the apostle Paul instructed Christians to "teach and admonish one another with all wisdom through psalms, hymns, and songs from the Spirit, singing to God with gratitude in your hearts" (Colossians 3:16). And many centuries before that, psalmists wrote songs of praise to the Lord for His goodness, mercy, and love.

Those who teach young children know that they more easily remember facts and ideas when they're put to music. Maybe that's why songs were so important to people in biblical times—and why they are still so important to us today. God wants us to remember His goodness and love, and He has wired us to remember what we hear and sing in songs.

In Revelation 7:9–10, the apostle John writes of a day when uncountable multitudes will gather before Jesus for the greatest musical celebration of all time. But we don't have to wait until heaven to sing praise to our Lord. We can sing anytime, anywhere, an old song or new—with gratitude in our hearts.

Father in heaven, I thank You for the gift of music. When I need to feel closer to You, help me to remember that songs of praise will draw me ever closer to Your heart.

GIVING

God loveth a cheerful giver.
2 CORINTHIANS 9:7 KJV

A wonderful old saying that's been around pretty much forever goes something like this: "Don't throw out the baby with the bathwater." That's solid advice. In fact, we might suggest that you don't throw out the baby at all!

Few things in this world slosh around in more greasy, gray bathwater than the subject of money and giving. And while giving involves much more than just money, the baby in that proverbial tub is a treasure from heaven that deserves to be rescued and cherished. A truly generous heart can change everything for the better in ways that are hard to imagine.

Giving is dear to God's own heart—John 3:16 says He *gave* His own Son for us. And Jesus made this promise to us: "Give, and it will be given to you. A good measure, pressed down, shaken together and running over, will be poured into your lap. For with the measure you use, it will be measured to you" (Luke 6:38 NIV).

That verse sounds a lot like the Father's challenge to the Old Testament Israelites: "Bring the whole tithe into the storehouse, that there may be food in my house. Test me in this. . .and see if I will not throw open the floodgates of heaven and pour out so much blessing that there will not be room enough to store it" (Malachi 3:10).

When it comes to giving, God says, *"Test me."*

Today's verse has been steeping in lukewarm tub-tea for quite a while—it's time to take back everything the enemy has tried to suck down the drain. So what are you waiting for? *Test God today*. Give cheerfully, and see what happens.

Thank You, Lord, for giving. Help me to do the same.

IMITATION

He who says he abides in Him ought himself also to walk just as He walked.

1 JOHN 2:6 NKJV

In his book *Quiet Strength*, pro football Hall of Famer Tony Dungy says, "I love coaching football, and winning a Super Bowl was a goal I've had for a long time. But it has never been my purpose in life. My purpose in life is simply to glorify God."

A former head coach of the Tampa Bay Buccaneers and the Indianapolis Colts—with whom he became the first black head coach to win the NFL championship—Dungy is a great example of 1 John 2:6. He practiced what he preached. Dungy was patient and kind to his players, coaches, friends, and family. His style was different from many other coaches we see on the sideline—Dungy never yelled, cursed, or talked down to his players or coaching staff. He knew that the way to gain people's respect wasn't to belittle or embarrass them but to treat them the way he wanted to be treated. . . to imitate Jesus in the way He interacted with others.

It's so easy to get caught up in the behaviors of the people around us. We often imitate the world rather than imitating Christ. Unfortunately, when we do that, we lose credibility as Christians—our testimony is tainted and people don't see Jesus in us.

The apostle Paul wrote, "Imitate me, just as I also imitate Christ" (1 Corinthians 11:1). Or, today, imitate Tony Dungy as he imitates Christ—and bring yourself closer to living out 1 John 2:6.

Father, I pray that every day I will make the choice to imitate You, not those around me. May I find favor in Your eyes rather than in the opinions of my peers. Amen.

CREATION

For since the creation of the world God's invisible qualities—his eternal power and divine nature—have been clearly seen, being understood from what has been made, so that people are without excuse.

ROMANS 1:20 NIV

The world is full of creators, and you enjoy their movies, books, music, and art of all sorts. These artists create because they were made in the image of their Creator. Every time you marvel over a movie that brought you to tears or music that makes your spirit soar, realize that that small taste of genius isn't even a sampling of God's majesty and creation.

In fact, creation is so expressive that Romans 1:20 says it's evidence for God's existence—enough evidence that nobody can make an excuse for disbelieving: "Although they *knew* God, they neither glorified him as God nor gave thanks to him, but their thinking became futile and their foolish hearts were darkened" (verse 21, emphasis added).

As Christians, we recognize God's role in all of

creation and specifically in our own lives. But life can be distracting, and we can always use a refreshing reminder of His wisdom and goodness.

Every time you pack up your fishing gear and head to the lake, you can find God. On a walk through the park with your wife, you can find God. When you drive into a thunderstorm or a beautiful sunset, you can find God. You just need to remember to look.

Today, why don't you put down your phone, turn off the TV, and head outdoors for a bit. Stop. Look. Listen. Breathe. God is waiting for you in His creation.

Father, I don't unplug often enough to get out into Your creation. I want to make doing so a part of my regular routine.

REST

"Come to me, all you who are weary and burdened, and I will give you rest."
MATTHEW 11:28 NIV

The suffering of African American slaves in the United States has been well documented. Many were beaten and their families torn apart. Some were kept in conditions worse than the slaveholders' animals. It's no wonder that many tried to escape from such cruelty.

But imagine the stress of traveling hundreds of miles, often on foot, to reach a land that offered freedom. Consider the anxiety, while seeking food or shelter, of knocking on doors that may or may not be safe.

Thankfully, there were those who helped the weary and burdened slaves. Frederick Douglass, a freed slave in Rochester, New York, was one of them. He personally helped around four hundred fugitives to make their way from the southern United States into Canada. Along the treacherous trail to freedom, slaves faced threats at every turn. Being caught could mean death. But Frederick

Douglass—and the other heroes of the Underground Railroad—provided assistance and rest.

God does the same thing for His people. In Old Testament times, the psalmist wrote that "He will cover you with his feathers, and under his wings you will find refuge; his faithfulness will be your shield and rampart" (Psalm 91:4). When Jesus came, He made the beautiful promise we now know as Matthew 11:28.

Jesus never pretended that His followers would escape the troubles of this life. But He guaranteed that if we turn to Him, He will provide us with much needed rest.

Lord, I thank You for being a safe harbor in life's troubles, that in You I can have peace and rest.

JOY

Then my soul will rejoice in the
LORD and delight in his salvation.
PSALM 35:9 NIV

When it was launched in 1931, the USS *Indianapolis* was destined for history. But no one could have known that the ship would experience the greatest single loss of life in U.S. Navy history.

After delivering parts for the atomic bombs that would end World War II, the *Indianapolis* was torpedoed. Some three hundred sailors went down with the ship, while the rest were thrust into shark-infested waters.

Because of the top-secret nature of its mission, nobody knew where the *Indianapolis* was—or that it had been sunk. The disaster was not discovered until three and a half days later, when an American plane happened across the wreckage. Of the 1,195 sailors on the ship, only 316 were pulled from the water.

Twenty-year-old marine Edgar Harrell was one of those survivors. For days after the sinking, even as comrades were dying around him, he focused on God. Thinking of his family and girlfriend (who would later become his wife), Harrell prayed and recited verses to keep his sanity. And then he heard it—the sound of an airplane. The sound of rescue.

Decades later, the ninety-three-year-old Harrell told an interviewer, "There's not a day that goes by—many, many times a day—I just look up and say, 'Thank You, Lord!' "

Christians can live in the same kind of joy that Harrell experienced. Our joy doesn't depend on what's happening right now. Our joy is in the Lord and the salvation that He has given us—even when we're treading water with sharks.

Lord, may I feel the joy of my salvation. Keep me from focusing on my circumstances when I should be content with my eternal security in You.

WORTHY

I therefore, a prisoner for the Lord, urge you to walk in a manner worthy of the calling to which you have been called.

EPHESIANS 4:1 ESV

Many websites offer advice on achieving success in the workplace. And many of their suggestions for impressing the boss or getting along with coworkers appear to be simply common sense. Occasionally, though, a site offers counsel that goes against the expected—for example, the concept of "No Task Is Beneath You." This brief but powerful statement changes the workplace dynamic from serving a particular individual to serving the greater good.

Theoretically, we can all agree that this counsel applies to the Christian life. But as with C. S. Lewis's wry comment on forgiveness ("Everyone says forgiveness is a lovely idea, until they have something to forgive"), it's easier said than put into practice. Whether at work or play or church, many of us like to seek the big title or flashy role. Or at least we like to criticize those with the big title or flashy role. The reality, though, is that only a small number of people are gifted enough to lead an organization, dominate their hobby, or head a church. Truly, most believers are tasked by God to minister in humble, simple circumstances.

To be found worthy of our calling—to serve as a prisoner of the Lord, as the apostle Paul described himself—we must be willing to accept the idea that "No Task Is Beneath Us."

We love the unlovable in Jesus' name.

We serve the undeserving in Jesus' name.

We seek out the ignored and abused for Jesus' sake.

In doing so, we walk in a manner worthy of God's calling.

Father, may You find me living my best for You. May I be found worthy of my calling.

REFUGE

Trust in him at all times; ye people, pour out your heart before him: God is a refuge for us.
PSALM 62:8 KJV

Growing up in the shadows of the Alps, it's no wonder that Heinrich Harrer loved mountain-climbing and skiing. His skills afforded him many opportunities for adventure, including the chance to scale a twenty-six-thousand-foot Himalayan peak.

Unfortunately, Harrer's journey to climb Nanga Parbat occurred at a bad time for him. World War II had started, and since he was from Adolf Hitler's native Austria, Harrer was arrested by British soldiers and placed in a prisoner of war camp.

Harrer attempted to escape numerous times, finally succeeding with the aid of a friend and a yak. Ill-equipped for the formidable landscape of Tibet, Heinrich's party set out on what would become a twenty-month journey. After encountering bears, leopards, and thieves along the way, they finally arrived in tattered clothes at the gates of the forbidden holy city of Lhasa. Outsiders were not welcome, but there was no other place to go. Would they be admitted?

Few of us will ever flee across a frozen Tibetan plateau, but we are often exposed to the hard "weather" of life. Our journeys can be uncomfortable, exhausting, and dangerous. But there is good news: God promises to "cover you with his feathers. He will shelter you with his wings. His faithful promises are your armor and protection" (Psalm 91:4 NLT).

Harrer and his friend were eventually given sanctuary in Lhasa. God, in His great mercy and love, longs to be *our* refuge in all of life's circumstances.

Lord, You are the refuge that I seek.
Thanks for always having a place for me.

SWEET

Gracious words are a honeycomb,
sweet to the soul and healing to the bones.
PROVERBS 16:24 NIV

If you've watched TV news over the past several years, you might have found yourself disheartened by the negative tone of modern political discourse. No longer do people of opposing political parties treat one another as those with whom they disagree but still respect. Now, more often than not, political adversaries treat each other as enemies. And it seems there are no limits to the terrible things they'll say to or about their opponents.

Most people know that "sweet" words—comments that build up, comments that lead to peace, comments that heal hearts and relationships—are what the world needs. But it seems that fewer and fewer people speak them.

What would the apostle Paul say? "Do not let any unwholesome talk come out of your mouths, but only what is helpful for building others up according to their needs, that it may benefit those who listen" (Ephesians 4:29).

It's not always easy to speak gracious words. It can be hard to offer "sweet" words because, frankly, some people just don't deserve them. But as people God calls to be beacons of light in the darkness, we Christians shouldn't focus on what others *deserve*. Let's remember what God has done for us in dealing with our own sins through Jesus Christ.

Loving others as God loved us means a lot of things, including this: speaking love and grace into the lives of people He has put in our orbit.

God of healing, may the words I speak bring comfort and not hurt, reconciliation and not division. Help me to use wisdom and self-control when I speak so that I can glorify You and build up others.

LIGHT

Again Jesus spoke to them, saying, "I am the light of the world. Whoever follows me will not walk in darkness, but will have the light of life."

JOHN 8:12 ESV

The Festival of Tabernacles (also known as the Festival of Booths) was the third and final annual commemoration in which the ancient Jews would make a pilgrimage to Israel. The festival was held to remember Israel's time in the wilderness when the people lived in tents. It coincided with the celebration of the fruit harvest, during the autumn months. Lights on lampstands would be placed around the temple to provide illumination for dancing and other festivities.

During part of the festival, two priests would walk from the temple to the gates while blowing trumpets. When they reached the gates, they turned to face the temple and proclaimed that there had been a time in Israel's history when the nation worshiped the sun—but now they worshiped only the Lord.

This is the background for the speech that Jesus gave in John 8:12–59. During a festival where light plays such an important role, Jesus claimed to be "the light of the world." To an audience that once worshiped the sun, the Son of God had come to give light where it was most needed. Jesus' claim was audacious. . .but He was the only one qualified to make it.

We don't have to live life in the dark—Jesus invites us into His light. And when we have His light inside us, we can see exactly what we need to see, both how to live to please God and how to shine His truth on others.

---

*Lord, help me to walk in Your light.
Thank You for being the light of the
world. May I worship Your light alone.*

NEARNESS

The L*ORD* *is near to all who call upon Him, to all who call upon Him in truth.*

PSALM 145:18 NKJV

As Christians, our primary goal should be to seek God, to be near Him. He is our ultimate destination! Often, though, we feel inadequate or unworthy, and without the blood of Jesus, we are. But because of the Lord's sacrifice, we have an invitation to approach the Father and stay near Him.

Psalm 145:18 gives us a directive, however, in our manner of approach. We are to "call upon Him *in truth*." In other words, our approach must be pure, without ulterior motives. We should only desire to be closer to God, and that only for His glory. "Nearness" is not about selfish gain, with us thinking we can get something out of God. After all, James 4:6 tells us that He "resists the proud, but gives grace to the humble."

Our goal for growing close to the Lord should resemble that of the apostle Paul's desire for nearness to God.

As he wrote to the believers in Philippi, he wanted to "know Him and the power of His resurrection, and the fellowship of His sufferings, being conformed to His death, if by any means, I may attain to the resurrection from the dead" (Philippians 3:10–11). It didn't matter what happened to Paul himself—all he wanted to do was grow closer to his Lord.

And that's how *we* draw closer to God too. Through humility, at any cost, calling upon Him "in truth."

Lord, I seek You sincerely. My soul desires You and my flesh longs for You because Your ways are good and Your love is true.

PURPOSE

We know that God causes everything to work together for the good of those who love God and are called according to his purpose for them.
ROMANS 8:28 NLT

During a reconnaissance mission in World War II, Louis Zamperini's bomber crashed into the Pacific Ocean. He and two other crew members survived the impact and were able to secure a raft from the wreckage. During the next forty-seven days, as Louis floated in shark-infested waters, he declared that if he were rescued, he would serve God with his life.

Louis was rescued but not as he anticipated: Japanese sailors captured and mistreated Louis before he was sent to a prisoner of war camp for the next two years. When freed at war's end, he finally returned to the United States. Haunted by nightmares of his experience, he turned to alcohol. Louis became violent, picking fights with strangers. His wife prepared to file for a divorce.

But when she heard Billy Graham speak and accepted

Christ, she changed her plans—now she wanted to get her husband to hear the up-and-coming evangelist too. Louis went and remembered his promise while adrift in the ocean. He surrendered his life to Jesus, ultimately becoming an evangelist. He even returned to Japan and preached the Gospel to the Japanese soldiers who had tortured him!

We all have times when life feels beyond our control. And we all wonder at times what our purpose is. But God is always working, whether we see it or not. As the prophet Jeremiah quoted Him, "I know the plans I have for you. . . . They are plans for good and not for disaster, to give you a future and a hope" (Jeremiah 29:11).

Lord, may I have patience as You work out Your purpose for my life.

SUCCESS

"Keep this Book of the Law always on your lips; meditate on it day and night, so that you may be careful to do everything written in it. Then you will be prosperous and successful."

JOSHUA 1:8 NIV

As front man for the iconic grunge rock band Nirvana—one of the biggest acts of the 1990s—Kurt Cobain seemed to have everything a young man could want. But in spite of his fame, money, wife, and baby, Cobain suffered from depression and drug addiction. Having lost all hope, in April 1994 he took his own life. He was twenty-seven years old.

Sadly, there are many stories like Cobain's—of young, successful people who "have it all" but can't go on in this world. Countless others work themselves to exhaustion trying to achieve what the world calls "success." But instead they find what King Solomon, in the book of Ecclesiastes, called "vanity."

God wants His people to do well, but His promise

for Joshua to be "prosperous and successful" was made with a condition: obedience to the divine law. That's something that still applies to Christians today. When we commit ourselves to the promises and commands found in God's written Word, the Bible, He commits Himself to us. God will give us what we need to be the people He wants us to be and do the things He has called us to do.

That's the kind of success we should all seek.

Lord God, thank You for your promise of success in this life if I only hold to Your Word. Help me always to remember that while You bless some people with what the world calls "success," real success means becoming all that You created me to be.

FORGIVEN

"Blessed are those whose transgressions are forgiven, whose sins are covered. Blessed is the one whose sin the Lord will never count against them."

ROMANS 4:7–8 NIV

"Make one mistake and you pay for it for the rest of your life": immortal words spoken some fifty years ago by the famed beagle (and occasional World War I fighter pilot) Snoopy of Charles M. Schulz's comic masterpiece *Peanuts.*

Everyone makes mistakes. And some of us make more than others. But creating lists of those mistakes and reviewing them again and again gives our enemy a tremendous foothold. Give the devil an inch, and he'll go the extra mile to destroy every good thing in your life—preferably from the inside out.

Like the Red Baron, Satan is always lurking just out of sight. He's looking for any opportunity to fill your trusty Sopwith Camel full of big, black bullet holes and send you hurtling toward the ground. You know, with smoke pouring out of your banged-up backside.

So what can you do when the devil hits the mark—when you crash and burn all over your family or friends or coworkers. . .again? In those times it's important to remember that Jesus really did pay it all. Forgiveness is purely a gift but if we want it, we have to reach out and take it.

Are you worried that you've messed up one too many times? That it's too late? That you could never be forgiven? If so, cheer up. You haven't just been forgiven, you've been *blessed*. You are the man whose sin—all of it—the Lord will never count against him again.

Jesus, thank You for paying the penalty my sins deserved. The past is gone. My sins are gone too. I can start over, forgiven.

Bible Wisdom for Men entries were written by

Bob Evenhouse: pages 22, 32, 42, 54, 78, 102, 106, 112, 120, 136, 142, 152, 166, 168, 172, 186, 192, 200

Zech Haynes: pages 8, 18, 44, 68, 124, 134, 146, 162, 182, 198

Josh Mosey: pages 6, 30, 36, 48, 86, 88, 98, 114, 126, 140, 154, 158, 164, 188, 196

Paul Kent: pages 26, 64, 96, 160

Phil Smouse: pages 28, 40, 50, 74, 84, 92, 118, 128, 180, 204

Tracy Sumner: pages 12, 20, 34, 58, 60, 70, 80, 104, 108, 144, 156, 170, 178, 194, 202

Lee Warren: pages 10, 14, 24, 38, 46, 62, 66, 72, 82, 90, 100, 110, 116, 122, 130, 138, 150, 174, 176, 184

Russell Wight: pages 16, 56, 76, 94, 132, 148, 190

Steve Wilson: page 52